DEVELOPING
ROOTS & WINGS

**A Trainer's Guide to
Affirming Culture in
Early Childhood Programs**

STACEY YORK

Redleaf Press
a division of Resources for Child Caring

The author of this book, Stacey York, is an accomplished trainer, teacher and speaker on the subject of multicultural education in early childhood. You can arrange to have her speak, present or train with your organization by calling Redleaf Press at 612 - 641 - 6631.

Redleaf Press would like to thank the International Institute of Minnesota for the use of their photos of textiles that appear on the cover. Included are textiles from Hmong, Native American, Ukranian, French and Near East cultures.

© 1992 by Stacey York

Published by: Redleaf Press
                  a division of Resources for Child Caring
                  450 North Syndicate, Suite 5
                  St. Paul, Minnesota 55104

Distributed by: Gryphon House
                  PO Box 275
                  Mt. Rainier, Maryland 20712

ISBN: 0-934140-75-8

Library of Congress Cataloging-in-Publication Data

York, Stacey
     Developing Roots & wings : a trainer's guide to affirming culture in early childhood programs / Stacey York.
          p.   cm.
     Companion to the text, Roots & wings.
     Includes bibliographical references.
     ISBN 0-934140-75-8
     1. Early childhood education—United States—Activity programs—Handbooks, manuals, etc.   2. Intercultural education—United States—Activity programs—Handbooks, manuals, etc.   3. Curriculum planning—United States— Handbooks, manuals, etc.
I. York, Stacey, 1957- Roots & wings.   II. Title
III. Title: Developing Roots and wings.
LB1139.35.A37Y67 1992
372.19—dc20   92-11974

Printed in the United States of America.

TABLE OF CONTENTS

Session 5: Cultural Diversity through the Classroom 99

Session 6: Planning Multicultural Curriculum 109

Session 7: Simple Activities You Can Use to Teach
Multicultural Awareness 123

Session 8: Multicultural Holidays and Celebrations 137

Session 9: What's the Difference? A Child's Perspective of Race 151

Session 10: Culturally Responsive Child Care 173

Session 11: Talking to Children about Differences 195

Appendix: Affirmation Symbols 206-208

Bibliography 209-210

Handouts

Author's Note and Dedication

I am like many of the early childhood teachers who attend my workshops and classes. I was an average to poor student in elementary, junior high, and high school. Teachers complained that I was too shy, left-handed, and didn't apply myself. I, too, have many negative memories of school—memories of teachers wanting me to be different, memories of being bored, memories of being afraid to ask questions, and memories of teachers being mean (really mean) to other kids. And I had mixed feelings about continuing my education beyond high school.

Fortunately, something very positive happened to me in college. Like my parents, I attended the local community college. I had wonderful teachers and I learned a lot. Having a positive adult learning experience increased my self-confidence and allowed me to see myself as someone who was capable of learning and understanding.

Five years later, I returned to college. I completed an undergraduate degree at a major university. It was a very trying experience, as this bureaucracy was not set up nor interested in meeting the needs of working adults. I found the research and information fascinating, but the professor's arrogance and distance from the real world of early childhood classrooms (particularly day care) disturbing. I will always remember one female professor shaking her head and saying, "Yes, Stacey, I don't think you want to go to graduate school here. You are too 'applied.' "

The small size and informality of graduate school was like a breath of fresh air. I was allowed to write in my own voice—not "collegese." Classes utilized a variety of teaching formats so that students were active and had choices, unlike the hours of lecture I endured at the university. Here I learned how to be reflective, dialogue, and think for myself. What a gift!

I strongly support adult education. Positive adult learning experiences helped me believe in myself. The community college gave me the tools to learn, a basic understanding of children, and some very practical job skills. The university helped me learn about research, taught me how to work systems, and endure. Graduate school gave me a chance to experience active-adult learning. It also allowed me to realize that I am a clear thinker and I have good ideas, even though I'm a shy left-handed day dreamer who still transposes letters, confuses numbers, and can't spell worth beans.

As a result, this training manual is dedicated to all the teachers who affirmed and challenged the learner in me. In doing so, I affirm the important role of all adult educators and trainers. And I recognize now that it was the little things, the interpersonal relationships, and the individual attention that mattered to me.

My kindergarten teacher, Miss Garcia, who was so nice.

My fifth grade teacher, Mrs. Ralston, who read the Laura Ingalls Wilder books to us every day after lunch.

My sixth grade teacher, Mr. Stillwell, who loved my drawings.

My eighth grade art teacher, Mr. Zuniga, who entered my ceramic dog in a contest.

My eleventh grade child development instructor, Mrs. Reardon, who got me excited about working with young children.

Mr. Robbins and Mr. Kennedy, the student body cabinet advisors, who helped me learn about leadership, budgeting, and parliamentary procedure.

My English Composition 101 instructor at Saddleback Community College. She was a part-time extension instructor, and the evening course was offered off campus during the summer. I wish I could remember her name because she taught me how to write sentences, paragraphs, and essays. She was the first person to tell me I could write.

Sally Sanger and Dennis Hudson, community college early childhood studies instructors, for giving me a solid foundation in early childhood education.

Howard Williams, professor of adult education, for telling me my work was inspired.

Shirley Moore, professor of child psychology, for opening up her personal library to me and telling me I could do graduate-level work.

Louise Derman-Sparks, Karen Fite, Betty Jones, Arwin Larkin, Elizabeth Prescott, and Niki Trumbo, graduate school teachers, who provided me with an empowering, holistic, active-learning experience. I would have never thought learning could be so fun! Thanks.

Why Is Multicultural Education Important?

Multicultural education and multiculturalism is a trend whose time has come. I once heard James Garbarino, President of the Erikson Institute for Advanced Study in Child Development, say, "America could always be counted on to do the right thing, after it had tried everything else." It is nearly thirty years after the civil rights movement and little has changed. After generations of trying to strip Native Americans of their culture, destroying the African-American culture, and shaming immigrants into hiding their culture, America may be ready to do the right thing. It's time to wake up and realize that America is a universal nation and that in less than ten years, one third of the country's population will be people of color. Expecting people of color to strip themselves of their culture and assimilate into American culture is arrogant and foolish. America must do the right thing and embrace a new strategy for achieving a united society.

Multiculturalism and multicultural education provides each of us in early childhood education an opportunity to work toward creating a truly democratic society that acknowledges, affirms, and utilizes the strengths and gifts of each of its cultural groups.

What Is Multicultural Education?

Multicultural education is a thoughtful, strategic response to a democratic and pluralistic society that continues to perpetuate racism. This approach focuses on what is happening in the United States today. Multicultural education in the early years should not focus on global awareness, and multicultural activities should not teach children how to take a foreign vacation.

What Is the Purpose of Multicultural Education?

The purpose of multicultural education is twofold. First, it is a strategy to prevent and eliminate the development of prejudice and racism in children. We have a window, a sensitive period, during the first nine years of a child's life. This is the time to teach children trust, acceptance, and respect. Children must be allowed to notice differences and taught to recognize the similarities among the members of their community. It is also the time to challenge children's distorted or pre-prejudice thinking.

Second, I hope that children will learn how to live cooperatively with people who are different from themselves. The early years are the years in which we need to help children develop a positive racial identity, cultural awareness, and social skills. From this foundation, which multicultural education provides, we can move on to help children become free of all biases and prejudices.

An anti-bias approach logically follows multicultural education. Multicultural education helps children acquire the ability to notice and accept racial differences. It gives them basic skills in forming friendships with people who are culturally different from themselves. An anti-bias approach allows the curriculum to be expanded to address the variety of prejudices against people that are present in contemporary American society, whether it is sexism, classism, ageism, handicappism, or homophobia. An anti-bias approach helps children to identify unfair situations and teaches them how to work together to challenge prejudice and injustice. This approach is also age-appropriate for young children, and it is based on years of thoughtful research and practice. (Derman-Sparks, 1984)

Once children are older and have the social/emotional skills to recognize and accept diversity, we can introduce a third type of learning experience. Children ages 7-12, who are in Piaget's concrete operations phase, are ready to learn about other countries and cultures. A global awareness approach is developmentally appropriate for this age group and should be added to the curriculum along with anti-bias and multicultural education.

Unfortunately, many teachers only think of multicultural education in terms of global and cultural awareness. This approach becomes the tourist approach when watered down to meet the needs of young children in early childhood settings. Sometimes, teachers are afraid of addressing diversity issues in their classrooms and turn to the tourist approach as a way to provide multicultural education and maintain their comfort level. This is an example of reactionary decision-making, which likely will result in children strengthening their stereotypes and pre-prejudice behavior.

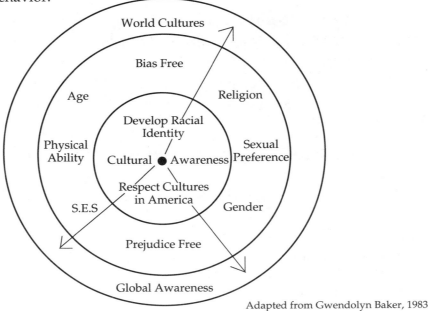

Adapted from Gwendolyn Baker, 1983

Why Is Training Important?

I've been conducting multicultural education workshops for five years and college courses for two years. Since *Roots and Wings* was published, I've traveled around Minnesota presenting workshops for early childhood educators. As a result, my thinking has become clearer and my conviction stronger. It's the workshop participants' stories, comments, and questions that lead me to believe multicultural education and training teachers to implement multicultural education is an absolute necessity.

Teachers Are Confused

Time and time again I meet teachers who want to do what's right, who don't want to make a mistake. Teachers don't want to offend parents or coworkers, and they don't want to hurt children's feelings. For this reason, they choose to ignore the differences and teach children that everyone is the same.

Teachers Lack Knowledge

Many teachers lack a working understanding of multicultural education. When asked "What is multicultural education?" most say that multicultural education is learning about other cultures. Some might say it is learning about the cultural differences. Others will say that it is learning the traditions, customs, and languages of other cultures. When asked how they implement multicultural education, early childhood teachers describe elaborate cultural festivals, cooking activities, making costumes, learning another language, and singing songs in another language. Some teachers identify books, posters, and multicultural dolls as the way they teach cultural diversity. Yet most don't know what to do with those materials, other than set them out in the classroom.

A third question posed to the teachers reveals the confusion. I ask "Why is multicultural education important?" and the answer is usually right on. Teachers will say multicultural education helps children accept differences and get along with one another. Multicultural education is important to reduce racial tension or eliminate prejudice. Teachers can easily identify the goals of multicultural education: to accept and affirm differences, to teach social skills, and to eliminate stereotyping and prejudice. But teachers are confused as to how to achieve those goals in their classroom. They mistakenly think teaching about world cultures and holidays is the way to resolve domestic racial issues.

Teachers Lack Awareness

Teachers are also unaware of who needs multicultural education. Many early childhood teachers think that only teachers in culturally diverse programs need to implement multicultural education. They think that everyone is the same in their program or community—that there really aren't any differences or that they don't have any problems with racism or prejudice. Teachers need to understand that prejudice is pre-judging people. It is not based on personal contact. Human beings don't need to have personal experience with a person from another race to become racially prejudiced. If prejudice were actually based on personal contact, we would have a lot less prejudice. Besides, regardless of where we live—be it the city, suburb, or rural township—we live segregated lives, and few of us can say we have friends who are racially different from ourselves.

Teachers Don't Understand Development

Teachers don't understand the role of racial identity, cultural awareness, and prejudice in children's development. Most of us were never taught these topics when we took child development, and this information certainly isn't included in most child development text books. When teachers understand the stages of children's racial awareness, they can begin to understand why the tourist approach is developmentally inappropriate and why they need to begin with noticing differences and similarities, labeling physical characteristics, and comparing skin color. Labeling, matching, classifying, and seriating are what young children need to be doing. They do not need to learn history and geography.

This summer I conducted a two-hour training session with the staff of a public school, school-age child care program in a small town in rural Minnesota. The staff had recently offered an activity of making and eating chocolate ice-cream sundaes. The teachers called them "brown bear" sundaes, but the children insisted on calling them "nigger sundaes" and made numerous racial slurs about the brown ice cream. The all Euro-American staff didn't say anything. It wasn't until after a two-hour workshop on the development of prejudice in children that the staff realized this type of behavior is inappropriate and should be challenged.

The staff hadn't thought about prejudice much, especially since they were operating on the belief that everyone in their town was the same, and that Euro-American children need to be around African American children in order to learn racial prejudice. As a result of the training, they had some new awareness, and now they wanted to further explore how to act on that awareness. In other words, they wanted to figure out how to respond to incidents like this in the future. The staff members weren't sure what to say, and they knew they didn't want to remain silent. Other staff were now wondering what type of activities they should include in the curriculum to help children develop positive attitudes toward people of other cultures. Yet others were identifying more incidents that had occurred that illustrate the children's awareness of racial diversity and pre-prejudice attitudes.

The conclusion I come to time and time again is that children notice racial differences and begin to exhibit pre-prejudice behavior at a very early age. Most early childhood teachers don't understand the development of racial identity, cultural awareness, or prejudice. As a result, early childhood teachers tend to ignore children's inappropriate behavior, much less help children acquire accurate information and foster acceptance and respect for racial diversity.

Conclusion

The worst thing that can happen is for a program or training institution to offer a two-hour workshop on multicultural education. For the teachers whose eyes have been open, a two-hour workshop leaves them hanging with lots and lots of questions and nowhere to find answers. And for the teachers who aren't convinced that multicultural education is important , a two-hour workshop allows them to meet their program or states' inservice requirement without having to change or really look at themselves. My biggest fear is that teachers' attitudes will become, "Oh, multicultural education. I went to a workshop on that last year. I've had that already."

Teachers need accurate information and help clarifying the issues. Time and time again, Euro-American teachers come up to me after workshop sessions and say things like, "I'm so glad I came today. I learned so much. You've opened my eyes. I didn't think this topic pertained to me, but now I know that it does." When teachers become aware either through reading or training, it's like the tip of an iceberg has just been discovered. From that point on, each teacher is on her own journey of growth and discovery. Some teachers want to reflect on their own attitudes and upbringing. Some want to know more about working with culturally diverse children and families. Some want activity and curriculum ideas. Others want to know about holidays or how to talk to children about cultural diversity. We need to develop training programs that eliminate the confusion and are comprehensive enough to address the multiple needs of teachers attempting to implement multicultural education.

SECTION TWO

Why Use an Active Learning Approach to Multicultural Training?

The purpose of multicultural education training is to motivate teachers to implement multicultural education in their early childhood classrooms. The outcome of multicultural training must be informed action. My dream is that teachers will change their teaching style, transform their classrooms, and modify their curriculum. I'm looking for change—personal change, institutional change, and eventually societal change.

Teacher Knowledge, Attitudes, and Skills Related to Multicultural Education

Successful implementation of multicultural education requires three things: knowledge, attitudes, and skills. Knowledge refers to understanding concepts and ideas. Teachers need to know the terms, types of approaches to multicultural education, and the meaning of culture. Knowledge can be gained through reading, films, lectures, discussions, and observations. Attitudes describe how the teacher feels and the emotional response that accompanies her interaction with children, parents, and co-workers.

Attitudes are very difficult to change. Some adult education experts believe it takes two years to impact a person's attitudes. Stories, case studies, guided imagery exercises, and simulation exercises are examples of the types of activities that may be emotionally charged enough to prompt a teacher to examine herself.

Skills identify the specific techniques that a teacher uses in implementing a multicultural curriculum. Projects, demonstrations, role play, and make-it-take-it activities give teachers an opportunity to develop and practice new skills before trying them with the children.

Teach to the Whole Person

Just as early childhood education seeks to facilitate the development of the whole child, adult training experiences must teach to the whole person. Teaching to promote increased knowledge, attitudes, and skills in teachers is just like teaching to the cognitive, social-emotional, and physical development of the child. Ignoring one of these areas results in ineffective teaching. A teacher who has the knowledge and skills but displays a negative, judgmental attitude won't be effective at implementing multicultural education. Many teachers who implement the tourist approach have positive attitudes and good teaching skills, but they simply don't have a solid understanding of multicultural education. A teacher who understands the issues and is respectful, open, and flexible but doesn't have a clue as to how to implement multicultural education won't be effective either.

A multicultural teacher training program will need to be designed to incorporate the knowledge, attitudes, and skills involved in implementing multicultural education.

Multicultural Education Teachers Need:

Knowledge	Attitudes	Skills
professional roots	self-awareness	set multicultural goals
multicultural terms	aware of own biases	select an appropriate approach to multicultural education
meaning of culture	slow to judge others	develop implementation plan
importance of multicultural education	self-acceptance	identify, remove stereotypic materials
types of multicultural education	accept, respect diversity	create multicultural materials
institutional racism	courage personal responsibility	
process of implementing multicultural education	believe diversity is good	set-out, display multicultural materials
staff roles in implementing multicultural education	culturally aware	purchase multicultural materials
teacher steps in implementing multicultural education	value other cultures	plan and implement multicultural activities
teaching through the classroom environment	willingness to change	incorporate cultural diversity into unit themes
guidelines for selecting multicultural materials	willingness to take risks	individualize curriculum unit
types of multicultural materials for interest areas	willing and able to learn from own mistakes	plan and implement holidays and celebrations
types of multicultural visual displays	believe multicultural education is important	facilitate development of children's racial identity
sources of multicultural materials	flexible, adaptable	facilitate development of children's cultural awareness

Knowledge	Attitudes	Skills
multicultural unit themes	respectful	conduct enrollment meeting
curriculum planning process	cooperative	conduct parent conference
individualize curriculum plans	ethical, honest	demonstrate problem solving/compromising with parents
multicultural concepts children understand	empathic, sensitive	plan and implement parent involvement activities
skills children acquire through multicultural education	takes child's, parent's perspective	provide culturally responsive child care
types of multicultural activities	positive, enthusiastic	talk to children about differences
roles of holidays and celebrations in early childhood education	creative, innovative	use language to empower children
developmentally appropriate celebrations	shows initiative, motivation	use language to expand children's thinking
holidays and celebrations of other cultures	sense of humor	respond to children's questions
development of children's cultural awareness	professionalism	respond to children's discriminatory behavior
development of prejudice	open to children's questions	
effect of prejudice on children's development	appreciate support families	
child rearing patterns influenced by culture	trust	
child's need for continuity	patience	
culturally responsive child care		
parent involvement in early childhood programs	value ethnic pride	
problem solving		
role of language in multicultural education		
active listening and effective communications		

Sources: Feeney, Stephanie, Christensen, Doris, Moravcik, Eva. *Who Am I in the Lives of Children?* third ed. Columbus: Merrill, 1987. Feeney, Stephanie and Chun, Robyn. "Effective Teachers of Young Children," *Young Children.* November 1985. Baker, Gwendolyn C., *Planning and Organizing for Multicultural Education.* Reading, MA: Addison Wesley, 1983.

Questions to Ponder

As you examine this chart, consider these questions:

1. How could a two-hour workshop on multicultural education prepare teachers to implement multicultural education in their classrooms?
2. What inaccurate ideas might teachers get from attending a two-hour workshop on the broad topic of multicultural education?
3. How would you organize a series of training sessions to cover this material?
4. What elements of multicultural education could be incorporated into existing training sessions/courses?

What Motivates Teachers?

As a trainer, what could you possibly do that would motivate teachers to implement multicultural education? After all, implementing multicultural education involves a complex set of tasks. It includes choosing an approach, identifying goals, strategizing how to reach those goals, removing stereotypic materials from the classroom, making multicultural visual displays, diversifying the curriculum, implementing multicultural activities, celebrating holidays in the context of the children's daily lives, talking to children about differences, promoting children's racial awareness, providing culturally responsive child care, and involving parents in the early childhood program.

Some Methods Don't Work

From experience I've learned that at least two methods don't work. Lecturing doesn't result in action. I can talk all day and not convince a single teacher that multicultural education is important, much less motivate her to implement it in her classroom. And I can't be the expert who comes in and does it for teachers. If I implement multicultural education for them, they'll never learn to do it for themselves.

Empowerment Leads to Implementation

Education for empowerment is an approach to adult education that results in action. When teachers are empowered, they take personal responsibility for their teaching practice. Education for empowerment …

means to encourage them to take control. Individuals who take control actively attempt to influence people and organizations affecting their lives. Empowerment is a process through which individuals gain skills and knowledge about themselves and their environment, which increases their confidence and enables them to exert control over their environment to effect desired changes. Ideally, fully empowered individuals are aware of their strengths and can effectively act on their own behalf. (Vanderslice, Virginia, Cherry, Cochran, and Dean, 1984, 1).

Methods designed to empower participants are also known as emancipatory education, issue-based curriculum, and reconstructionist education. Emancipatory refers to the process of freeing individuals to act for themselves. Issue-based education describes an emergent curriculum that comes from the participants own issues, questions, and concerns. This method is empowering because it relates directly to the participant's daily life. The title, reconstructionist education, reflects a learning process that results in teachers reconstructing their thinking, attitudes, and teaching practices.

Education for empowerment is a holistic approach. Like child-centered curriculum, it teaches to the whole person. Participants are empowered by increasing their knowledge and gaining new information. Empowering education includes an affective component that promotes self-awareness and attitudinal change. This occurs through personal and critical reflection. Empowering education supports action by providing an opportunity to practice skills and apply concepts. In terms of multicultural education, education for empowerment results in teachers taking informed and committed action.

Let's take a closer look at the role of information, personal reflection, and practical application in multicultural training.

Provide Current Information. Implementing multicultural education requires informed action. Accurate information reduces the possibility that teachers will react without forethought to the current interest in multicultural education. I believe the tourist approach is often such a reaction. Teachers need information—the most current, accurate information available. They need it presented in a way that is not overwhelming, too theoretical, and easily related to application. Teachers need knowledge that relates to their classrooms and their experiences with young children. Teachers may want to know how to tell if something is stereotypic. They may want information about multicultural activities or where to purchase resources. As a trainer, it is our role to help early childhood teachers acquire the information they need to implement multicultural education.

Facilitate Personal Reflection. Successful implementation requires personal reflection. It is through reflection that teachers engage with the information. They take it in and it becomes internal as teachers reflect on how the information relates to their own lives. Without reflection, knowledge about multicultural education remains someone else's ideas. We want teachers to play with the ideas, rearrange them, and make them their own.

Personal reflection also reduces the possibility that teachers will remain locked in their ignorance and denial. Shelby Steele calls it "selective ignorance" when people learn about the racial inequality in the United States and choose to deny that it exists or is relevant to their lives (Steele, 1990). Teachers, for example, may shut me out if I lecture at them on the importance of multicultural education. But teachers can move beyond ignorance and denial if I engage them in discussion and ask them about their personal experience.

The risk of critical reflection is "analysis paralysis." It is easy for teachers to become overwhelmed by the significance, size, and scope of multicultural education. This often happens when well-meaning directors hand their staff a book and say, "I want our program to be more multicultural. Read this and tell me what we should do." Analysis paralysis can be avoided if teachers are given a chance to practice applying multicultural concepts.

Practical Application. Practice makes perfect. Teachers need an opportunity to try out their ideas and related multicultural concepts in actual situations. A training program must give teachers a chance to make visual displays, try out activities on one another, plan a curriculum unit, or rewrite a parent intake form. *Roots and Wings* is not a recipe book approach to multicultural education. It is not a canned curriculum that tells teachers what to do step-by-step. The wonderful thing about this is that each teacher will implement multicultural education in his or her own way. Providing hands-on activities will help teachers take action in their own classrooms.

The Purpose of a Trainer's Guide to *Roots and Wings*

The trainer's guide is intended for trainers, directors, and college instructors. I wrote *Roots and Wings* because I saw a need for a resource book that was easy to read, organized in a way that made sense to teachers, and full of accessible, practical ideas. The multicultural curriculum described in *Roots and Wings* is worthwhile only if teachers can put it into practice. *A Trainer's Guide to Roots and Wings* is designed to help you, the trainer, provide an empowering adult learning experience that helps teachers implement multicultural education.

Roots and Wings is not a recipe book. It isn't a canned curriculum. It doesn't contain prescribed themes or scripted activities. *Roots and Wings* provides an introduction to early childhood multicultural education. It provides background information, guidelines for implementing a multicultural curriculum, and many activity ideas. This training guide serves as a resource that you can use to help teachers transform their classrooms and adapt multicultural curriculum to fit their situation.

The Risk of Texts

The greatest risk of planning a training program around a book is that the participants will become objects. When this happens participants passively receive information, and the content of the course becomes more important than the learners. This process can be especially damaging when the content perpetuates societal myths and stereotypes, or denies the participant's real life experiences. I don't want the information presented in *Roots and Wings* to become more important than early childhood teachers and the real children they serve.

A Trainer's Guide to Roots and Wings attempts to strike a balance between content-based and issue-based instruction. The class/workshop sessions presented in this guide accompany the information presented in *Roots and Wings* and use a format that facilitates education for empowerment. Topics of information are often presented as questions or problems to be solved. Exercises, journaling, and affirmations provide opportunities for teachers to increase their self-awareness and develop attitudes that support multicultural education. Each session includes activities to help teachers develop skills and practice implementing multicultural education.

Workshop Descriptions

This guide contains a descriptive outline for eleven separate workshops or class sessions. Each session lasts approximately two-and-a-half to three hours. You are encouraged to present the workshops as a series. The order of the workshops corresponds with the chapters in *Roots and Wings*. Sessions may be offered as an individual workshop series, or combined to create a three-credit course. Remember, please don't combine the workshops to create one session that attempts to cover everything!

Match Workshop Sessions with *Roots and Wings* Chapters

Roots and Wings	Workshop Sessions
Chapter 1: Introduction	Session 1: Roots and Wings
Chapter 2: What is Multicultural Education?	Session 2: What is Multicultural Education?
Chapter 3: Implementing Multicultural Education	Session 3: Beginning with Me: Racial Awareness for Teachers
	Session 4: The Do's and Taboos of Implementing Multicultural Education
Chapter 4: Teaching through the Classroom	Session 5: Cultural Diversity through The Classroom
Chapter 5: Activities for Teaching Children about Culture	Session 6: Planning Multicultural Curriculum
	Session 7: Simple Activities You Can Use to Teach Multicultural Awareness
Chapter 6: Holidays and Celebrations	Session 8: Multicultural Holidays and Celebrations
Chapter 7: Children's Awareness of Differences	Session 9: What's The Difference? A Child's Perspective of Race
Chapter 8: Culturally Responsive Care and Education	Session 10: Culturally Responsive Child Care
Chapter 9: Talking to Children about Differences	Session 11: Talking to Children about Differences

Class Format

Each workshop session presented in this manual provides you with the basic information needed to prepare and conduct a multicultural workshop. The workshop titles and descriptions can be used to promote and advertise the workshop. The goals listed for the sessions will help you prepare, select evaluation activities, and introduce the workshops to participants. All the sessions follow the same empowering educational process that includes an ice breaker, problem posing, presentation of content, critical reflection, practical application, journaling, and affirmations. Additional activities are included to provide flexibility.

Jagged Start

The first few minutes of a class session sets the tone for the rest of the session. Participants don't know what to expect when they enter the classroom. It's the trainers role to make everyone feel welcomed and at ease. Have the room arranged ahead of time so that you can greet participants as they arrive. Use what Elizabeth Jones calls a "jagged start." This means the trainer has an activity ready to go for participants as they enter the room. It may be completing registration, making a name tag, reading the course syllabus, introducing themselves to another classmate, or discussing some questions written on the chalkboard.

Bring the entire group together after 10 - 15 minutes and formally introduce yourself and the class session. If the class is small, consider asking everyone to introduce themselves. Group introductions help create a sense of community among the entire class. But skip it if there are 25 people in a two-hour workshop; otherwise you'll take up a half an hour on introductions alone. Review the title, description, goals, and ground rules to make sure everyone is in the right place. Introduce yourself and the group sponsoring the training.

A jagged start creates a relaxed atmosphere and allows participants to ease into the learning situation. It sets a tone of interaction and active learning. It rewards those who are on-time without penalizing the late-comers. Best of all, you won't have to repeat the course introduction twice.

Jagged Start

Goals:

    Participants are greeted as they arrive.

    Participants become oriented to the classroom and have time to get settled.

    Participants are awarded for arriving on time or are not penalized for arriving late.

    Participants experience a relaxed atmosphere.

Techniques: on the classroom door or chalkboard

        fill out registration or attendance forms

        make a name tag

        get refreshments

        read course syllabus, handouts

(Jones, 1986)

Ice Breaker

Sometimes you might want to plan more formal ice breaker or get-acquainted exercises during the jagged start. These games or small group discussions are the beginning of the adult learning process. In the first session, for example, participants begin by making a poster about themselves. In the second session, participants play a modified version of bingo.

Other times you could simply ask participants to find a partner or form a small group and discuss the questions you've written on the chalkboard. This allows participant to form relationships with one another right away. Ice breaker questions are designed to get participants talking about their personal experiences and interests. This way, the participants are invited to bring themselves into the classroom and become the subject of study, rather than focusing exclusively on some predetermined content.

Ice Breaker

Goals:

> Participants form relationships.

> Participants establish personal safety.

> Participants become active learners.

> Participants begin exploring the topic through their personal experiences.

Techniques: personal posters

> bingo

> culture sharing

> small group discussions

> sharing in pairs

> personal opinions

> storytelling

> reflecting on childhood experiences

Problem Posing

Next, formally introduce the workshop topic with a question or a problem to be solved. For instance you might ask, "What is a holiday? What is a celebration? Why do holidays and celebrations pose problems in early childhood programs?" Participants' own questions and concerns can also be the basis for problem posing. In this case you would ask the class, "What are your questions about multicultural education? What makes implementing multicultural education difficult?" In both of these instances, problem posing takes place as a large or small group activity.

Problem posing helps participants move from isolation to recognizing that many of their questions and concerns are common and are shared by other early childhood teachers. Problem posing, like ice breaker activities, allows participants to begin the learning process by naming their own experiences. By posing the topic as a question or problem, participants discover, on their own, that they need some new information. They need to know more if they are going to answer their own questions. This questioning stance sets a tone of learning as investigation, research, and examination. It prevents participants from quickly sliding back into the familiar student role of passively receiving information and memorizing facts.

Problem Posing

Goals:

Participants experience the topic as a question to be answered or a problem to be solved.

Participants identify and share their questions and concerns.

Participants recognize the common themes.

Participants realize they aren't alone.

Participants begin to see the complexity of the issue.

Participants realize they need more information.

Participants experience learning as investigating, researching, and examining.

Techniques: listing participants' questions, concerns about the topic posing questions

defining terms

body sculpting

guided imagery, visualization

nominal group technique

Presentation of Content

Once the participants are aware of their own experiences and how those relate to the topic of study, the class investigates the topic. The purpose of presenting content is to increase understanding and promote the development of a new consciousness.

A topic might be understood by connecting it to existing bodies of information. A topic like children's racial awareness may be explored by connecting it to child development theories. The topic of racism and prejudice could be connected to the social and political environment in which teachers live. Participants look to other perspectives and theories to offer a description, interpretation, or explanation.

This portion of a class session is like a search for the truth. While some technical information may be shared by you, there is also the opportunity for participants to recreate knowledge. Participants may increase their consciousness through analysis and further investigation. You may help the class expose myths, challenge assumptions, and identify contradictions.

Presentation of content gives participants an opportunity to fully understand their situation and prepares them to take informed action. They learn theory in a practical sense, as it relates to their life. This dynamic process allows participants to participate in the creation of knowledge, think critically, and have their own "ah-ha" experience.

Presentation of Content

Goals:

Participants increase their understanding of a topic.

Participants expose myths, challenge assumptions, identify contradictions.

Participants have a cognitive "ah-ha" experience.

Techniques: brainstorming

mini-lectures

guest speaker or panel discussion

small group discussion

large group discussion

reading

interviews

observations

watching a video

cognitive webbing

document review

Critical Reflection

This step of the learning process takes the topic out of the intellectual "clouds" and brings it back to the participants' life experiences. Critical reflection challenges participants to relate to the topic personally. It focuses on affect, attitudes, and interpretive knowledge whereas presentation of content emphasizes intellectual knowledge and critical thinking.

Critical reflection provides participants with an opportunity to engage in self-examination and increase self-awareness. You provide experiences that draw out the teacher's feelings and give them an opportunity to reinterpret their situation. Participants may identify the feelings associated with their experience, reflect on past behavior and attitudes, create new images, examine possible solutions, and identify strategies for action. For example, participants might evaluate their own classroom, discuss case studies, or answer the question "What can you do on behalf of multicultural education?" These experiences promote sensitivity, insight, and attitudinal change. Critical reflection is absolutely crucial because the personal soul searching involved motivates participants to take action.

Critical Reflection

Goals:

Participants relate new information or understanding to their own experience.

Participants examine their attitudes and intuitive feelings.

Participants reflect on past behavior and attitudes.

Participants generate possible solutions and action strategies.

Participants become motivated to take action.

Techniques: priority setting

case studies

questionnaires

guided imagery

checklists

rating scales

relate one situation to another

self-assessment

evaluate unit themes, or multicultural activities

Practical Application

The learning experience cannot end with critical reflection. It would be disempowering to take participants through a consciousness-raising process and in effect say, "Now you are aware. You are on your own from here." Participants would be left feeling overwhelmed and discouraged.

Practical application combines knowledge, personal reflection, and action. It focuses on the individual, giving each teacher a chance to use her new knowledge for herself. Practical application provides a supportive environment in which participants can experiment with adaptation, implementation, and change. Above all, it is the essence of empowerment, which Carr and Kemmis describe as "informed, committed action which is based on wise and prudent practical judgement about how to act in this situation" (Carr, W. and S. Kemmis, 1986, 190).

An empowering trainer offers activities that bring the learning back to the concrete daily lives of the participants. Making plans, implementing activities, creating materials, and rewriting a parent intake form are examples of experiences that occur during the practical application phase of the learning process. For instance, in one session participants plan and implement a multicultural activity for young children. In another class session they practice responding to children's questions about differences. Practical action allows participants to refine their skills, develop strategies, and make materials.

Practical Application

Goals:

Participants combine new knowledge with personal reflection to create informed action.

Participants practice adapting, implementing, and making change.

Participants experiment in a supportive environment.

Participants have an opportunity to use the knowledge, attitudes, and skills gained for themselves.

Techniques: case studies

role playing

problem solving

participant presentations

making teaching aids

writing a position statement

implementing an activity

implementing a curriculum unit

Journaling

I was first introduced to journaling as a student at Pacific Oaks College. Teachers provided each student with a file folder. Sometimes we journaled in class, sometimes on our own as an assignment. Journals were turned in to the instructors who read and responded to them. If the class was very large, instructors had students read and respond to each other's journals.

Journaling provides a powerful way for participants to reflect on their own experience. By reading and responding to the participants' journals, the trainer has a chance to develop an individual relationship with each participant, support her thinking, and encourage her to go deeper in exploring the material.

Try to ease participants' initial apprehension by telling them you don't have a red pen and you don't care about their spelling or sentence structure. Let them know you are interested in their thinking and how the class is going for them. If a participant has difficulty with spelling and grammar, you might want to ask her for permission to make corrections. After all, the goal of journaling is self-awareness and critical reflection.

Journaling

Goals:

Participants reflect on their own experience.

Participants are challenged to think critically.

Participants experience an individual relationship with the trainer.

Affirmations

Affirmations are another powerful learning tool and they are an effective way to change attitudes and behavior. These constructive statements affirm a teacher's thinking, attitudes, and behavior. As a form of self-talk, affirmations create a positive attitude within the participant. With a positive attitude, a teacher feels reassured and confident, and is motivated to take meaningful action.

Affirmations create a new reality. They are always stated as though they are true today, in the present. The affirmation "I respect all families," for example, is stated as though it is a way of being, whereas the statement "I will respect all families" remains lost in the future. When an affirmation is read, it replaces the old negative and self-defeating messages.

Next, the positive thinking, attitude, or behavior is envisioned. The teacher sees herself as she wants to be (in this case respecting families). Visualizing something, like multicultural education, causes teachers to believe that it is possible. If a teacher believes in multicultural education, she is much more likely to put forth the effort to make it a reality.

Affirmations

Goals:

Participants develop positive internal self-talk.

Participants establish and maintain a positive outlook that motivates them to take action.

Participants visualize change and new possibilities.

Each session includes a list of affirmations specifically related to the content presented in that workshop session. Duplicate and distribute the affirmations to participants. You could also use them as examples and ask participants to write their own affirmations. If that's the case, follow these general guidelines for writing affirmations.

1. Begin each affirmation with the word "I."
2. Write the affirmation in the present tense.
3. Keep the affirmation positive, simple, and specific.

A set of symbols are included in this manual. There is one symbol to accompany the set of affirmations in each workshop. Reproduce the symbols on bright colors of card stock and distribute them to participants. Ask participants to cut out the symbols and write an affirmation on each one. The collection of affirmations will increase with each workshop. They can be stored in a plastic jar or some other type of decorative container that can be kept in the classroom. Each day the teacher draws an affirmation from the jar, reads it, and meditates on it through the day.

There is another way to use the symbols and affirmations. Reproduce the symbols on colorful card stock. Have participants cut each sheet of symbols into four rectangles. Write an affirmation on each rectangle. Punch two holes at the top of the rectangles and secure them with two metal rings. This makes a spiral "book" of affirmations. The teacher can read one affirmation a day, flip it to the back, and read the next affirmation the following day.

Additional Activities

Numerous additional activities are included with each session. These activities make the training guide very flexible and allow you to adapt the workshops to meet your needs. Use them to create your own workshop or extend the workshop to an all-day or two-session workshop by incorporating some of the additional activities into the agenda. Many of the additional activities are very effective in individual training like CDA or in consulting with individual programs. A combination of these activities might also be given as assignments and used to evaluate teacher competence or assign a letter grade.

SECTION THREE

The Trainer's Role

Your role as a teacher trainer is extremely important. Effective trainers acknowledge, call forth, and nurture the experience and individuality of each teacher. It is our responsibility to create a safe, accepting atmosphere and set participants at ease. We function as resource people who help teachers expand their self-confidence, knowledge, teaching skills, and caregiving skills. As we facilitate discussions, we must communicate clearly and effectively, and lead the class through the empowering learning process.

A Midwife-Teacher

The trainer's role in empowering education is similar to the teacher's role in an early childhood classroom. The focus is on fostering participant empowerment by structuring and facilitating an active learning experience. The empowering trainer joins with the participants in this learning process. Problem posing, group discussions, and brainstorming activities create a partnership between the participants and the trainer. Together they learn from one another.

As many early childhood teachers know, it is important to nurture children's curiosity and good ideas. The same is true with teaching adults. Recently, researchers in women's development have identified the type of adult educator that is most effective with women learners. They call this trainer a "midwife-teacher" and describe her as follows:

> They assist the students in giving birth to their own ideas, in making their own tacit knowledge explicit and elaborating it...Midwife-teachers do not administer anesthesia. They support their students' thinking, but they do not do the students' thinking for them or expect the students to think as they do...They encourage the students to speak in their own active voices...the Midwife-teacher's first concern is to preserve the students' fragile newborn thoughts, to see that they are born with the truth intact, that they do not turn into acceptable lies...Midwife-teachers focus not on their own knowledge (as the lecturer does) but on the students' knowledge. They contribute when needed, but it is always clear that the baby is not theirs but the student's.
> (Belenky et al. 1986, 217-218)

Understand Women's Thinking and Learning

Understanding how women learn is an important part of a trainer's role. Trainers need to be able to choose the most effective teaching strategies and presentation methods for their participants. Knowing how women learn and develop their thinking will help you foster early childhood teachers' development.

Recently a group of human development scholars collaborated on an extensive research project to further identify how women's thinking develops. (Belenky et al. 1986, 217-218) discovered that women's self-concept is interwoven with how they think about the world. In addition they found that women learn through dialogue—listening and talking. While "seeing" and "vision" are the common metaphors for intellectual understanding and thinking, women in their study consistently used the metaphor of "voice" to describe their process of intellectual growth.

The researchers were able to categorize the ways in which women think and process information into five different positions or perspectives. Each position is unique with its own sense of self, concept of truth, and learning style.

1. **Silence.** A woman immersed in this perspective doesn't think that she has a mind, voice, or self. If asked to describe herself, a woman might respond, "I don't know. Ask my mother or husband." Learners at this position are very concrete in their thinking. Content must focus on the here-and-now, what is happening in her classroom today. Modeling, demonstrating, and showing teachers individually how to complete a task are appropriate training strategies.

2. **Received Knowledge**. Learners immersed in this perspective believe that authorities are the only people capable of thinking and knowing. A woman at this position does not yet have an internal voice. She doesn't trust herself to know what to do in a given situation. She believes only others, defined as experts and authorities, have information. She looks to receive guidance from experts and will want you to tell her what to do. Group thinking and problem solving activities like brainstorming and cognitive webbing help teachers recognize that everyone is capable of thinking and solving problems.

3. **Subjective Knowledge**. Learners immersed in this position have become aware of and rely completely on their inner voice. A woman's knowledge and thinking is very subjective, based solely upon personal experience, hunches, and gut feelings. When asked to explain why she uses a tourist approach, a subjective thinker would respond, "The kids like it and it's fun." "It's what we did when I was in school." "My parents took me on a vacation to Mexico when I was a little girl and I learned so much." It is very difficult for subjective thinkers to let go of their own ways of caring for children and try more appropriate, proven methods. Activities such as creating theory from personal experience, explaining why certain methods work, and relating theory to actual practice can help subjective knowers trust and value professional early childhood practices.

4. **Procedural Knowledge**. Procedural learners silence and mistrust their inner voice and intuition. A learner immersed in this position processes information through rational and logical thinking. A teacher with this perspective is interested in learning about theories, procedures, and techniques. She may be interested in knowing about different approaches and will choose the most appropriate for her setting. She can consider individual needs and begin to individualize learning and caregiving. Guided imagery and critical reflection activities can help a teacher at this stage acknowledge her inner knowing. She may also enjoy problem solving, individualized curriculum planning, and exploring culturally responsive child care.

5. **Constructed Knowledge**. Women immersed in this position interweave their intuitive hunches with their rational thinking. They are able to think contextually rather than individually. They realize that what works in one setting doesn't necessarily work in another. Teachers at this position enjoy creating knowledge based on what they have experienced and what they know. Team projects and collaborating with others to rewrite policies and create new activities are enjoyable experiences for these teachers.

Incorporating Women's Construction of Knowledge into Training

These five perspectives are important information for you, with many implications for structuring adult learning situations. I find that most early childhood teachers process information at the second and third positions. Learning activities that encourage teachers to reflect on their own experiences and draw conclusions from their experiences builds confidence in their internal hunches. These types of learning experiences validate what a teacher already knew but never put into words.

Moving subjective thinkers to accept early childhood theories, procedures, and tasks is a much more difficult task. Recently, a Euro-American preschool teacher spoke up in a workshop I was giving. She refused to acknowledge racial differences in her classroom because she was afraid she would hurt the feelings of the one African-American child in her class. This woman had freckles and had experienced teasing as a child. She believed her room would be a safe place for all children if they just noticed the similarities. It was of no use trying to convince her of the importance of noticing differences, because she wasn't thinking logically—she was thinking intuitively. In this case a small group discussion with some procedural and constructed thinkers might have shaken her up enough. Subjective learners need lots of opportunities to listen to other perspectives.

Multicultural Education Requires Additional Understanding

Trainers who teach multicultural education need understanding. We need to understand ourselves, multicultural education, and the broader issues related to multicultural education. Self-understanding comes from examining ourselves, identifying our own biases, and working to eliminate those biases from our lives. Experiences like living in a racially-mixed neighborhood, directing a racially mixed child care center, volunteering with an African-American community development project in Mississippi, attending workshops, and reading have helped me become more aware, more sensitive, and more understanding. This is an ongoing process that never ends. I strongly believe that I must model what I teach. So right now I am examining my own language, fear of differences, need for control, acceptance of privilege, and racial isolation.

Knowledge of Multicultural Education

Training teachers to implement multicultural education requires a thorough understanding of the topic. I've had a variety of experiences working with programs who are implementing multicultural education, and I've watched other early childhood programs struggle with it. Another important way to learn about the subject is by reading books and articles. It helps me understand the history, variety, and current trends in early childhood multicultural education.

Understanding of Broader Social Context

Multicultural education must be viewed in a larger context, and you need to understand the broader societal issues related to this struggle. We must recognize how institutional racism, sexism, classism, ageism, handicappism, and homophobia operate in our society. This broader perspective allows you to view human development, human behavior, and learning in a social context rather than from an individual perspective.

Willing to Risk

Training teachers to implement multicultural education puts me on the edge, personally and professionally. Most early childhood teachers would rather learn about music, science, or dramatic play. As a result, sometimes my classes are cancelled because of lack of enrollment. Sometimes I feel like a voice in the wilderness.

The topic of multicultural education arouses strong feelings in both myself and participants. I find that even teaching child guidance is a breeze compared to teaching multicultural education. After all, I care passionately about multicultural education and I am paid to say things that teachers may not want to hear. As a result I witness racism and prejudice on a regular basis. Teachers get angry at me.

Sometimes I leave a session thinking that the entire early childhood community is racist and feeling overwhelmed by how far we have to go. I say these things not to discourage anyone from teaching multicultural education, but to prepare you and to encourage you to find ways to take care of yourself. Here are some things that work for me: learn to recognize defenses related to racism and prejudice, don't take on someone else's anger, stay clear about what I am and am not responsible for, vent my anger and frustration to trusted friends and colleagues, limit the number of workshops I do in a week or month, cry, take a hot bath and listen to music, talk to my dogs, read poetry by people of color for inspiration, attend films or lectures that will inspire and nourish me, and most of all try to focus on the participants and programs that "get it" and are taking solid steps to incorporate multicultural education.

What's Going On? Am I the Crazy One?

Survival as a multicultural trainer rests on being able to stay clear on the issues and keeping your own sense of reality. This can be especially hard to do when working with people who use distorted thinking or defense mechanisms. The 1991 World Series between the Minnesota Twins and the Atlanta Braves provides a good example of how some people use distorted thinking and defenses as a response to racism and prejudice. The Atlanta Braves fans cheered on their team by doing the tomahawk chop, chanting, wearing war paint and pretend Indian headdresses. Local American Indian organizations, human rights groups, and individuals voiced their disapproval of these antics. Protests were held prior to each Twins home game to call attention to and challenge this derogatory and offensive behavior.

Many of the Atlanta fans were surprised and astonished that their behavior was interpreted as offensive. Comments like, "What's all the fuss about? Gee, we're just trying to have a good time. We're not trying to hurt anyone. Why don't you lighten up?" illustrate their use of denial, ignorance, minimization, and rationalization as defense mechanisms. Some fans responded out of anger with name-calling and statements like, "I really have a problem with someone telling me I'm derogatory."

I can recognize the use of psychological defenses in this situation because I see it so often in the early childhood community. Teachers who want to hold onto their tourist approach to multicultural education rationalize their behavior. They say things like, "Oh, but it's so fun and the kids enjoy it. At least we're doing something." Many early childhood teachers deny the need for multicultural education: "Don't you think children are too young for this?" or "Everybody is the same here, we don't have those kinds of problems like you do in the cities," or "We just need to focus on self-esteem and similarities, and everything will be fine." Sometimes I bear the brunt of Euro-American teacher's anger about multicultural education, especially when it is mandatory. Teachers have said to me, "I don't see why I have to go to all of this trouble. It's just one more thing I've got to do," or "I hate to tell you, but this isn't new information. Do you really think you are going to change the world?"

Don't let the defenses such as denying, minimizing, rationalization, or blame confuse you. Recognize that the people who are using these techniques are feeling threatened and choosing to not take responsibility for the situation. Reflect their thinking and feelings back to them by using active listening. Use your voice and body language to de-escalate the tension in the room. Acknowledge the disagreement without trying to convince. Try to explain your truth in clear, simple language. Then continue on with the workshop.

A Few More Training Tips

Teaching adults is similar to teaching young children. A lot of thinking and planning go into designing the learning experience. Teachers first consider the developmental level and capabilities of their students. Then they set goals. The room is arranged, the schedule set before the learner sets foot inside the classroom door. Knowledge of the participants, the environment and routines provide the hidden structure of an empowering learning process for adults as well as children.

If you are new to adult education and teacher training, this section will help you see the big picture and consider the details involved in training teachers to implement multicultural education.

Avoid the "Quick Fix" Approach

Often, multicultural education training is presented as a one-time workshop. I am often asked to conduct an evening workshop on multicultural education in which I'm supposed to share numerous activity ideas and tell teachers how to implement multicultural education. Program directors and training coordinators may assume that a one-time workshop is enough is get teachers started incorporating multicultural education into their programs. This is a symptom of the quick fix mentality and as trainers, we need to recognize that a superficial overview may be more damaging in the long run. Rather than increasing teacher interest, a one-time overview may reinforce a teacher's current practices or the denial of the importance of multicultural education. In planning multicultural education training we must recognize that teachers...

> come with carefully constructed protective cocoons through which any new or different interpretation of reality must pass. Experiences that do not come with great force into and through that screen end up adding more layers to the cocoon. Experiences that have enough depth and duration and intensity to challenge the prevailing interpretation are therefore those that education for transformation seek to develop (Evans, Evans, Kennedy, 1987, 237).

Conduct a Preliminary Investigation

You will probably want to get some background information and take care of details prior to conducting a workshop. For instance, you may want answers to these questions: Who is sponsoring the workshop? What is the purpose in providing training? What are they hoping will happen as a result of the training? Who will participate in the session(s)? How many people will attend? What is the ethnicity of the participants? How much experience and prior training do they have in multicultural education? Answers to these questions will help you design and prepare a workshop to fit the participants' needs.

There are many details involved in conducting training. These nuts and bolts include setting a time, choosing a location, setting the participants' fee, and arranging for your payment. You may also want to ask the sponsors: Who is responsible for making hand-outs? Will refreshments be provided to participants? Is audio-visual equipment available? Who will set up the room? Will someone be there to meet me when I arrive?

Scheduling Workshops

Offer training at times that are convenient for early childhood teachers. Most day care centers are in operation from 6:00 a.m. to 6:00 p.m. Monday though Friday. As a result, training sessions should be scheduled for evenings after 6:30 p.m. or on Saturday mornings. Because many teachers must report to work early in the morning, sessions should not go beyond 9:30 p.m. You might also want to experiment with offering weekend classes. A twelve hour/one-credit course could be completed with a combination of Friday night, all day Saturday, and Sunday morning; or all day Saturday and Sunday sessions. This may be an effective way to serve teachers who must drive great distances to attend training classes. Weekend classes may be the only option for family child care providers. Consider offering training courses in conjunction with state and regional conferences.

Choosing a Classroom

Room arrangement and the classroom environment affects the participants' behavior and learning. Chairs set up in rows facing the same direction encourage participants to be passive learners and discourage group discussion. Chairs in a semi-circle or circle, or tables that seat four participants encourage discussion and participation. This guide offers activities from a variety of formats such as: small group discussion, role play, brainstorming, individual journaling, and mini-lecture. Select a room with flexible seating that can be rearranged for both small group and large group activities. Also make sure that the classroom allows participants to move around. An auditorium setting is very difficult to work with and should be avoided if at all possible.

Consider Environmental Aesthetics

Pay attention to the aesthetics of the room. Seating should always be adult-sized and comfortable. Look for rooms that have blank wall space for posting the agenda, chart paper, and showing films. Make sure the room is quiet and free of distraction from noise. Ventilation is also important. Realize that as a trainer, you may become so engrossed in conducting the workshop that you won't notice the temperature or air quality in the classroom. Choose a classroom with manual thermostatic controls when conducting an all-day training session.

Light is another key factor to consider in the selection of an adult classroom. Personally, I find it very difficult to read in a room lit by fluorescent lights. I also think and reflect more easily in rooms with windows. No space is perfect, but try to find a classroom space that supports your methods.

Materials and Equipment for the Adult Classroom

flip chart	overhead transparencies
newsprint	glue
chalkboard	scissors
chalk, eraser	name tags
felt tip markers	television or VCR monitor
crayons	VCR
overhead projector	

Provide Closure to Each Session

Drawing the session to a close is just as important as taking the time to start the class off on the right foot. Abrupt endings leave adults hanging, unsure of what happened, and not knowing what comes next. Take the last 5 - 10 minutes to wrap-up the class with a summary of the main points of the class session, affirmation of the group process and participant, and an invitation to continue thinking about the topic at hand. Depending on the class, you may ask participants if they have any questions or comments about the session. Homework assignments can also be presented at this time. Use the closing moments to prepare students for the next session by briefly stating the topic and any special activities such as a guest speaker.

Ending the last session of a course can involve summarizing the course content, reflecting on class experiences, providing the participants with feedback on their participation, and completing an evaluation. You may also want to provide one final experiential activity to reinforce the topic and create a heightened sense of accomplishment and satisfaction for the participants. Sometimes a class will just "click." When this happens acknowledge it by celebrating the energy, enthusiasm, and effort that has taken place over the past weeks. A dessert potluck or sharing a meal together are two ways of celebrating and building on the success of the class.

Possible Activities

group game

small group-sharing of what the course has meant to them

write a letter to yourself and don't open it for a year

affirmation poster—each person has a piece of newsprint with their name on it, posted on classroom walls. Participants and trainer write notes and draw pictures on each others posters.

*Adapted from Elizabeth Jones, *Teaching Adults: An Active Learning Approach*. Washington D.C.: NAEYC, 1986.

Course Evaluation

Participants in early childhood teacher training sessions will represent a wide range of educational experience and ability. Some may have a high school diploma, others a GED. Some will have completed vocational training through technical college or community college, others will have a CDA. Some will have baccalaureate degrees. Recognize that school may not have been a positive experience for some teachers. Negative feelings, low self-esteem, and lack of self-confidence may accompany these adult learners into the training sessions. In addition, older participants may feel anxious because it has been many years since they were in a formal learning situation.

Nowhere is it more important to maintain a sense of trust and safety than in the evaluation process. Create evaluation procedures that offer participants an opportunity to evaluate themselves. Consider using qualitative rather than quantitative forms of assessment. This trainer's guide does not include formal tools such as an exam, but there are several additional activities included with each session outline. Use these activities to assess participants' learning or create your own assessment materials.

Possible Activities

> pre- and post-test
> narrative self-evaluation
> observation of a child
> group project
> individual project
> videotape of teaching
> checklist

Evaluating the Course and Trainer. Teaching a course includes conducting an evaluation of the course and trainer. Design an evaluation tool to meet your specific needs and distribute it at the end of the last class session. Have all participants fill it out and drop it off at a designated place as they leave. Completing evaluations empower participants by giving participants a chance to acknowledge their experience. Let participants know when course changes have been made as a result of feedback received on the evaluation forms. The evaluation process also empowers trainers, as we receive written feedback on our teaching style and presentation of material. You can use the evaluation information to debrief after a class and refine the workshop for future use.

Using Course Evaluation Forms

1. Pass out the evaluation form just before the end of the last class.
2. Create evaluation forms to give you the information you want.
3. Keep the evaluation forms anonymous.
4. Encourage providers to give honest, detailed answers.
5. Use the feedback to make changes in the course structure or your teaching style.

Guidelines for Leading Large Group Discussions

Large group discussions don't happen automatically. Large group discussions are successful when many people contribute their ideas, feelings, and experiences. Group discussions help participants decenter and view situations from other perspectives. Keep in mind the following guidelines when preparing and leading large group discussions:

1. Know the purpose of the discussion.
2. Ask thought-provoking questions.
3. Demonstrate "with-it-ness." Be aware of the group dynamics.
4. Serve as a bridge by relating participants' comments.
5. Take notes of the main points.
6. Close the discussion with a brief summary.
7. Transition the group into the next activity.

Guidelines for Facilitating Small Group Discussions

Small groups usually range from three to ten people. Small group discussions are particularly useful in training early childhood teachers because they provide a smaller, safer environment for sharing ideas, thoughts, and feelings. Participants get more time to talk and are not as intimidated because the trainer is not present leading the discussion. Consider the following guidelines when using small group discussions:

1. Give clear and specific directions.
2. Tell groups where to meet and remind them to sit in a circle.
3. Vary the way you divide the class into small groups.
4. Tell the groups how to record their discussion if you want them to report back to the whole class.
5. Be available to answer questions, move about the room, and listen in on discussions.
6. Provide groups with five and two minute warnings that the discussion is about to end.

*Adapted from *Communication for Empowerment: A Facilitator's Manual for Empowering Teaching Techniques* by Vanderslice, Cherry, Cochran, Dean. Ithaca: Cornell University Press, 1984.

Recommended Reading

Here is a list of books that will help you learn more about education for empowerment and facilitating adult learning.

Arnold, R., D. Barndt, and B. Burke. *A New Weave: Popular Education in Canada and Central America*. Toronto, Ontario: CUSO/Ontario Institute for Studies in Education, 1986.

Arnold, Rick and Bev Burke. *A Popular Education Handbook*. Toronto, Ontario: CUSO/Ontario Institute for Studies in Education, 1983.

Auvine, Brian, Betsy Densmore, Mary Extrom, Scott Poole, Michel Shanklin. *A Manual for Group Facilitators*. Madison, WI: The Center For Conflict Resolution, 1977.

Bateman, Walter L. *Open to Question*. San Francisco: Jossey-Bass Publishers, 1990.

Belenky, Mary Field, Blythe McVicker Clinchy, Nancy Rule Goldberger, and Jill Mattuck Tarule . *Women's Ways of Knowing*. New York: Basic Books, Inc., 1986.

Coover, Virginia, Ellen Deacon, Charles Esser, and Christopher Moore. *Resource Manual For A Living Revolution*. Philadelphia: New Society Publishers, 1977.

Diamondstone, Jan M. *Designing, Leading and Evaluating Workshops for Teachers and Parents*. Ypsilanti, MI: High/Scope Foundation, 1980.

Evans, Alice Frazer, Robert A. Evans, and William Bean Kennedy. *Pedagogies for the Non-Poor*. New York: Maryknoll, 1989.

Freire, Paulo, and Ira Shor. *A Pedagogy for Liberation*. South Hadley, OH: Bergin and Garvey Publishers, 1987.

Freire, Paulo. *Education for Critical Consciousness*. New York: Continuum Publishing Corp., 1973.

_____. *Pedagogy of the Oppressed*. New York: Continuum Publishing Corp., 1970.

_____. *The Politics of Education*. South Hadley, OH: Bergin and Garvey Publishers, 1985.

Horton, Miles, and Paulo Freire. *We Make the Road by Walking*. Philadelphia: Temple University Press, 1990.

Jones, Elizabeth. *Teaching Adults: An Active Learning Approach*. Washington D.C.: National Association for the Education of Young Children (NAEYC), 1986.

Katz, Judith H. *White Awareness: Handbook For Anti-Racism Training*. Norman, OK: University of Oklahoma Press, 1978.

Koberg, Don, and Jim Bagnall. *The Revised All New Universal Traveler*. Los Altos: William Kaufman, 1981.

Murdock, Maureen. *Spinning Inward*. Boston: Shambhala, 1987.

Newstrom, John W., and Edward E. Scannell. *Games Trainers Play*. New York: McGraw Hill Book Company, 1980.

Shor, Ira. *Critical Teaching and Everyday Life*. Chicago: University of Chicago Press, 1987.

_____ ed. *Freire for the Classroom*. Portsmouth: Boynton/Cook Publishers, 1987.

Vanderslice, Virginia, Florence Cherry, Moncrieff Cochran, and Christiann Dean. *Communication for Empowerment*. Ithaca: Cornell University, 1984.

Roots and Wings

Description

An introductory session for individuals who are interested in giving young children their cultural roots and the wings to soar beyond prejudice and discrimination. Get to know one another, explore the concept of "roots" and "wings," learn how multicultural education fits into the field of early childhood education, and familiarize yourself with the terminology of multicultural education.

Goals

1. Experience a warm, safe, and trusting atmosphere.
2. Establish relationships among participants.
3. Begin identifying participant's interests, awareness, and skill levels.
4. Review the course and textbook.
5. Identify professional roots and current trends related to early childhood multicultural education.
6. Identify and define terminology associated with multicultural education.
7. Recognize assumptions regarding multicultural education.

Ice Breaker: Personal Posters   45 minutes

Prior to class, set out a selection of crayons, felt tip markers, and colored pencils. Write the directions for the opening activity on the chalkboard for all to see.

Welcome to Introduction to Multicultural Education!

Please print your name on the name tag and put it on so we know who you are. Take the large piece of paper and make a personal poster. Use drawings, words, and/ or symbols to tell us about yourself. Include a few things most people don't know about you.

When you are finished making your poster, tape it up on one of the walls in this room.

We will get together for group time in fifteen minutes.

Stacey

As participants enter the classroom, greet them and give them a name tag and a large piece of drawing paper (12" x 24" or larger). If they have trouble getting started, refer them to the information on the chalkboard and paraphrase the instructions.

After about fifteen minutes, gather the group together. Ask participants to introduce themselves using the poster they made. Depending on the time and situation, you might also ask participants to share their reasons for taking a class on multicultural education. You may want to make a personal poster yourself or have one already made that you can share with the group.

Consider collecting the posters and storing them. At the last session, have the participants create another poster and compare the two as a way of identifying changes that occurred as a result of the course.

Introduce the Class   30 minutes

Course Content

Ask participants: "What topics would you like us to talk about in this class? What do you want to learn about, related to multicultural education?" Write their responses on chart paper so that everyone can see the list and you can save it for future reference.

Pass out a class schedule or syllabus. As you introduce the course, show the participants where and when their concerns will be incorporated in the class. Clearly introduce and explain any assignments, grades, and/or evaluations.

Your Teaching Style

Decide ahead of time how you want to describe yourself as a trainer/instructor. Do you want to share your educational background? your work experience? your interest in multicultural education? When are you available to participants? How can they reach you? Also describe your teaching style so that participants will know what to expect. Here's what I might say:

Each session will be very much like today has been. We will use a variety of formats: individual work, small group discussions, large group discussions, and lecture. I will try to vary the activities to meet the needs and interests of everyone. So we'll read, journal, brainstorm, role play, observe, interview people, evaluate materials, and design activities.

As a group, decide on the classroom, seating arrangement, and presence of food. Sometimes these are choices, sometimes they are not. I allow adult learners to have food in class. Sometimes classes decide to have a potluck at each session, have a group meal at the last class, or that participants will bring food for themselves if they are hungry.

The Textbook

Roots and Wings is an introductory text. That means it tries to cover all the major aspects of implementing multicultural education in an early childhood setting. It also raises important issues related to multicultural education. It is divided into nine chapters, and we will go through the entire book in this course. Tell participants if and when they will need a book, where to get it, and the cost.

Participants who are not used to taking courses may need a brief introduction to reading a textbook. Tell them:

It can be easy to get lost when reading a textbook. Use the subheadings to help you follow the author's line of reasoning. Subheadings are the bold print that stands above the text and they can also be found in the table of contents. Try taking notes on the reading and/or using a highlighter to mark the passages if you have a difficult time retaining the information and it seems like the words go in one ear and out the other. Others find it helpful to skim a chapter briefly to get the "gist" and then read it more thoroughly a second time. You may want to pair up with someone and form reading partners, especially if you have difficulty reading.

The Training Institution

Identify and describe the purpose of the sponsoring agency. Briefly highlight any services that may be of interest to participants and tell them how to get further information. Relay any policies or procedures (such as attendance, breaks, parking, and smoking) that participants need to know. Point out the location of the bathrooms, vending machines, pay telephones, and any other relevant areas.

Participants' Questions

Acknowledge that you have just covered a lot of important information in a very short amount of time. Ask participants if they have any questions about the course. Assure them that they can ask questions at anytime.

Problem Posing: Roots and Wings   10 minutes

> *There are two things that we can leave*
> *to our children...one is roots...the other, wings.*
> —Anonymous

Write the "roots and wings" saying on a chalkboard or distribute a copy of it to each of the participants. Read it aloud. Generate a group discussion of it. What is it? What is it saying? What does it mean? What does it say about the role of adults in children's lives? Why do you think the book was given this saying as its title? How do "roots" relate to multicultural education? How do "wings" relate to multicultural education?

Presentation of Content   15 minutes

Roots and Wings of Early Childhood Education

Present a mini-lecture on the heritage of early childhood education and current trends within the field to provide a context in which to place early childhood multicultural education. Use pages 11-15 as a guide and include additional historical influences and current trends that are important to you. Use recent census data and national, state, and local events to illustrate support for multicultural education and barriers that prevent incorporating cultural diversity into our programs.

Terminology   **30 minutes**

Review the list of terms on pages 18-19 in *Roots and Wings*. Ask yourself, "Are there any additional terms that I want to introduce to participants?" Depending on the participants' level of awareness, you may want to add words to the list. Here are some examples: colorblind,white privilege, entitlement, bigot, selective ignorance, white innocence, culturally invasive, racial integration, racial segregation, racial desegregation, integration shock, racial identity, demoralization, cultural complementarity, personal responsibility, racial equality, white guilt, cultural dynamics, justice, human rights, culturally responsive, racial insensitivity, and multiculturalism. Prior to the session, print each word on a separate index card and gather together a few dictionaries.

As we learn about multicultural education in the weeks to come, we will be using a number of words or terms related to multicultural education. It will help our group communication and your understanding of the reading to clarify these terms. Shuffle the cards and pass one out to each participant. One by one, ask participants to say the word, define it, describe how they feel when they see the word before them, and relate any experiences they've associated with the term. Set out the dictionaries so that participants can look up any words they are unsure of or that raise questions.

Continue the inquiry into the terminology of multicultural education by asking these questions: Who decides which words are important for you to know? Are there any words that have been left out that you would like to add to the list? Who decides what these words mean? Which words seem loaded—that is, have hidden or multiple meanings? What causes them to mean different things to different people? How do our attitudes or feelings toward a word influence our thinking? How do our experiences with a word influence our attitudes or feelings about it?

Refer participants to the terminology list on pages 18-19 of *Roots and Wings*. Encourage them to write in additional words or definitions to make the list their own. Suggest that they can refer to it throughout the course.

Critical Reflection: Letter to the Reader   **15 minutes**

Tell your class:

Today we have explored the "roots and wings" saying, reviewed the foundation of early childhood education, and defined terms associated with multicultural education. Each of you are probably beginning to form some ideas about how all of this fits together. The author of Roots and Wings *has thought a lot about the relationship between herself, early childhood education, and multicultural education.*

Encourage the class to compare their ideas about themselves, their roles as teachers, and multicultural education with those of the author. Ask participants to read "A Letter to the Reader" on pages 9-10 and look for the themes in the author's life.

Once the participants have finished reading, discuss the letter. What is the author's experience? What do you think she is trying to say? Does it give you any more clues as to why the book is titled *Roots and Wings*?

If so, what are they? Tell participants that by identifying someone else's development they may be able to predict, anticipate, or gain new understanding of their own growth process as teachers implementing multicultural education. Ask participants to generate a list of themes from the letter. Write the themes on the chalkboard. The list of themes may look something like this:

importance of family
importance of cultural heritage
protection and support of children
empowerment, acting on beliefs
gaining perspective on discrimination
self-awareness
personal growth
discovering, naming your cultural identity
fear
isolation, sheltered
denial of differences
change

Next, draw a horizontal line across the chalkboard. Using the group's list of themes, ask the participants to sequence the themes in chronological order. Analyze the sequence. Ask: What does it tell us about her growth process? What might you want to look for in your own process of learning to implement multicultural education?

Practical Application   20 minutes

Guided Imagery

Use the following guided imagery with your students. Say:

Make yourself comfortable in your chair. Roll your shoulders backwards in a circular motion a few times and let your arms fall loosely in your lap. Close your eyes and take three deep breaths. As you exhale imagine that you are sending the tension and concerns of the day out of your body.

*

Imagine yourself a tiny being that needs to be inside a protective covering so that it can continue to be nourished and grow. Place yourself in this protective space. You may imagine yourself in a bubble, an egg shell, a cave, a womb, or surrounded by light. Take a minute to think about how you as a teacher of young children would like to grow and change so that you can effectively implement multicultural education in your classroom.

*

Know that you have everything you need to bring multicultural education into harmony and union with your values, teaching style, and the rest of your curriculum. Look inside yourself for the answers.

Where in your body is your emotional self? Focus your attention there and feel your emotions. Notice any discomfort you are feeling. What is it? How is it holding you back?

*

Where in your body is your intuition? Focus your attention there. Allow your intuition to lead you. Where is it pulling you?

*

Where in your body is your impulsive, energetic self? Focus your attention on this part of you. What does it have to offer you?

*

Where in your body is energy to relate to others? Focus your attention on the part of you that seeks human interaction. Imagine yourself talking and sharing freely with others.

*

Find your control button, that part of you that needs to be in control or have everything under control. Be the protective adult to your controlling self. Reassure this part of you that it's all right to let in some new or different ideas.

*

Focus once again on yourself as a young, growing being. What new sense of purpose would you like to acquire? What new things would you like to explore? Remember, you can go back to your protective space at any time. All parts of you: your mind, your emotions, your intuition, your physical/energetic self, and your social self are available resources to help you explore this material. When you are ready, leave your protective shell, join me in this room, and open your eyes.

A Letter to Myself

Give each participant a plain piece of paper and an envelope. Ask them to write a letter to themselves. Offer these questions as a guide or create your own questions: What is important to you? Who do you want to be as an adult who works with children? What do you know about yourself? What role do culture, race, and discrimination play in your life? Do you want to learn anything new regarding multicultural education? If so, what do you want to learn? Do you want to change? If so, how do you want to change? If you don't want to learn or change, why not? You can also suggest that participants reread "A Letter to the Reader" if they are still unsure about what to write.

Tell participants to fold their letters, seal them in the envelope provided, and write their name on the outside of the envelope. Collect the letters and return them to the participants at the last training session.

Journaling

These questions also appear on page 20 of *Roots and Wings.*

1. What people, theories, or life experiences have influenced what you do with young children?
2. What are your dreams for society? What impact do you want to have on children, families, or society?
3. What are your assumptions about multicultural education for young children?

Affirmations

Symbol: leaf

1. I am present and open to learning from this class.
2. I have a way of learning that works for me.
3. I am learning about multicultural education.
4. I recognize and set aside my assumptions about multicultural education.
5. I let go of my fears of multicultural education.
6. As a teacher, I am rooted in the early childhood tradition.
7. I ground my teaching in child development.
8. I affirm the goodness and uniqueness of each child.
9. I teach children about the real world.
10. I recognize that I live in a culturally diverse country.
11. As a teacher, I work toward social reform.
12. I am creating a peaceful, cooperative world for all children.

Additional Activities

Interview

Tell participants to interview five early childhood teachers outside of this class and write down their response to the interview questions. Discuss and analyze the responses in the next class session.

Early Childhood Teacher Interview Form

1. In your opinion, what are the traditions of early childhood education?

_____

_____

_____

_____

2. Do you think there is a need for multicultural education in early childhood?

_____

_____

_____

_____

3. Why or why not?

_____

_____

_____

_____

4. What are the barriers to incorporating multicultural education in early childhood programs?

_____

_____

_____

_____

Observation

Ask participants to use the following form to conduct an informal observation of their program to identify elements that either promote or hinder multicultural education. Divide the class into small groups so that participants can present their findings to one another.

Observation Record

Observation Site_____ Date _____

Observer _____

Item	Yes	No	Not Observed
Elements of the early childhood tradition			
1. Children are respected.	_____	_____	_____
2. Children are treated as individuals.	_____	_____	_____
3. Children are involved in the learning process.	_____	_____	_____
4. Staff teach to the whole child.	_____	_____	_____
5. Children learn through play.	_____	_____	_____
6. Curriculum content focuses on the present.	_____	_____	_____
7. The program attempts to improve children's lives.	_____	_____	_____
Elements of a global approach			
8. Staff recognize cultural differences.	_____	_____	_____
9. Staff prepare children to live in a culturally diverse country.	_____	_____	_____
10. Prepare children to live in a peaceful, cooperative world.	_____	_____	_____
Support for multicultural education			
11. Program is accredited by the National Academy of Early Childhood Programs.	_____	_____	_____
12. Staff are familiar with the anti-bias curriculum.	_____	_____	_____
13. Staff take workshops or read books on multicultural education.	_____	_____	_____
Barriers to multicultural education			
14. State licensing standards do not require/acknowledge multicultural education.	_____	_____	_____
15. Staff use "recipe books" exclusively.	_____	_____	_____
16. Staff choose activities because they're fun and entertaining.	_____	_____	_____
17. Staff use ditto sheets.	_____	_____	_____
18. Staff present craft activities.	_____	_____	_____
19. Animated characters are used to decorate the room.	_____	_____	_____
20. Photographs or posters of real people are absent from the classroom.	_____	_____	_____

Review Center Accreditation Procedures Criteria

Read through the Criteria for High Quality Early Childhood Programs in *Accreditation Criteria and Procedures of the National Academy of Early Childhood Programs.* Identify the goals statements and criteria that address multicultural education.

Review State Licensing Standards

Obtain a copy of your state's licensing standards for early childhood programs and/or staff. Review the standards. Is multicultural education mentioned? Is it a required component of early childhood programs? Is it listed as an acceptable teacher training course? Is it required for teachers? How do the current standards support multicultural education? How do the current standards serve as a barrier to implementing multicultural education? Who is responsible for writing and deciding upon the state standards?

What Is Multicultural Education?

Description

Do you know what multicultural education is? Here is an opportunity to learn about culture, examine culture's influence on children, identify the five main approaches to multicultural education, and set your own goals for multicultural education.

Goals

1. Identify the role of culture in children's lives.
2. Understand the importance of multicultural education.
3. Examine five approaches to multicultural education.
4. Relate teaching methods and outcomes to different approaches.
5. Write goals for multicultural education.

Ice Breaker: Multicultural Education Bingo   15 minutes

Distribute a "Cultural Awareness" bingo card to each participant. Tell them that the object of the game is to get a row initialed—either up and down, horizontally, or vertically. Any class participant can initial a square if the item names his life experience. But a person may only initial one square per bingo card. Remind participants to shout "Bingo!" when they've completed a row. You may need to encourage participants to get up and move around in order to get the game going. The game can be over once someone gets bingo or you may decide to keep it going to see who comes in second or third place. You might also ask the winners to verify their signatures as a way of helping the participants get to know one another.

Cultural Awareness Bingo Card

I teach children about their own culture.	I play music from another culture.	This is my first class on multicultural education.	I work in an integrated program.
I help children recognize differences & similarities.	I celebrate a holiday from another culture.	I have read a novel or book of poetry by a person of color.	I didn't see a person of color until I was eighteen.
I speak a second language.	I work in a segregated program.	I know a staff member that tells racial jokes.	I display multi-ethnic pictures in my classroom.
I know about my own ethnicity.	I have traveled to another continent.	I read folktales to children.	I help children challenge unfair situations.

Problem Posing   30 minutes

Brainstorm: What is Culture?

Facilitate a large group discussion based on the question "What is culture?" List participants' answers on the chalkboard. Refer to a dictionary if the class is unsure about their definition. Help the group further define culture. Say:

Now let's define culture in terms of three elements: things, traditions, and values/beliefs. These things are the concrete representations of a culture. They can be seen, heard, touched, or smelled. The traditions of a culture are the patterns, habits, and mannerisms that influence how people go about their daily lives. The values and beliefs of a culture determine its perspective on humanity and the world.

Draw three columns on the chalkboard. Label the columns things, traditions, and values/beliefs. Ask the group to identify all of the things associated with a culture and write their list of items in the column labeled "things." Repeat this procedure with traditions and values/beliefs. See page 22 of *Roots and Wings* for an example of this exercise.

Small Group Discussion: Is Multicultural Education Important?

Ask participants to form small groups of three to four individuals. Refer to the chalkboard with the definition of culture and the columns identifying elements of a culture. Ask participants to consider this information as they discuss the questions: Is multicultural education important? and What might be some positive outcomes of multicultural education? After a few minutes, tell participants to read the section "Why Is Multicultural Education Important?" on pages 22-25 in *Roots and Wings*. Ask them to compare their ideas with the author's statement.

Presentation of Content   60 minutes

Mini-Lecture: The Five Approaches to Multicultural Education

Present a mini-lecture on the five approaches to multicultural education. Use pages 25-28 in *Roots and Wings* as a guide. Add examples from local programs and curriculum resource materials to illustrate each approach. For example, I use a local college laboratory school as an example for anti-bias curriculum, and the public school bilingual program as an example of bicultural/bilingual education. I display overhead transparencies of ditto sheets from a second grade class to illustrate the single group studies approach. I also pass around posters, bulletin board sets, and resource books that reflect the different approaches.

Video: Anti-Bias Curriculum

Show the videotape, "Anti-Bias Curriculum." This 30-minute video gives participants an opportunity to see one of the approaches to multicultural education in action. It is available for purchase from either Redleaf Press, 450 North Syndicate, Suite 5, St. Paul, MN 55104-4125 ((800) 423-8309) or Pacific Oaks College,

714 W. California Blvd., Pasadena, CA 91105 ((818) 795-9161 x 74.) Following the video, give participants an opportunity to respond and ask questions. You may want to facilitate a brief discussion with questions such as: What were the main elements of their approach? Why did they become involved in multicultural education? What are the goals of the anti-bias curriculum?

Critical Reflection: Case Studies   30 minutes

Ask participants to meet in their small groups. Then introduce the exercise by saying:

This activity involves reading and discussing four case studies. Each one briefly describes an early childhood program and its approach to implementing multicultural education. The goal of this activity is to help you relate theoretical approaches to teaching methods and daily practices. The questions that follow each case study will help you think about the strengths, weaknesses, and effectiveness of the different approaches.

Distribute copies of the case studies. Ask group participants to read and discuss each program.

Approaches to Multicultural Education

Case Study One: Happy Hearts Day Care Center

The Happy Hearts curriculum emphasizes promoting social development and high self-esteem. Teachers want children to interact with others and feel good about themselves as learners. The goals include making friends, using words instead of hitting, appropriately expressing feelings, allowing everyone to play, sharing toys, avoiding name-calling and teasing, listening to others, and taking turns. Teachers offer numerous open-ended activities to encourage creativity, self-expression, and individual uniqueness.

The teachers use unit themes to organize and plan the curriculum. One of their favorite units is "I Am Special." This theme is often offered in September as a way for each child to start off the year feeling important and to get to know the other children. Teachers display photographs of each child on the bulletin board. The wall above the art area has space for displaying one piece of artwork by each child in the classroom. Activities such as making handprints, feet prints, whole body drawings, and books about oneself reinforce the theme.

Each child has an "I Am Special" day in which that child gets to share with the class things that make him or herself special, wear a button that says "I Am Special," be the teacher's helper for the day, and choose that day's snack.

Questions

1. Which of the five approaches does this program use? Give three examples to back up your answer.

2. What are the strengths of this approach to multicultural education?

3. What are the weaknesses of this approach to multicultural education?

4. What might the long-term consequences be for a child who attends this program?

5. What would you add or eliminate from the multicultural education curriculum in this program?

Approaches to Multicultural Education

Case Study Two: Learning Lane Child Care Center

Learning Lane seeks to enrich children's lives by providing them with a wide variety of activities and events that would normally be outside of a young child's daily experience. Teachers at Learning Lane take great pride in their curriculum which is rich in content and variety. Curriculum themes include: dinosaurs, myths and legends, and pilgrims and Indians. Staff wanted to add more multicultural education to the curriculum so they decided to spend the entire summer highlighting cultures from around the world.

During "Japan" week children folded paper cranes, made straw paintings, folded paper fans, and made coolie hats. They flew kites outside and played with rice in the sensory table. A Japanese prop box was set out in the dramatic play area offering children a chance to wear Japanese robes, getas, and have pretend tea parties. Each day, a snack was served that included tempura, mandarin oranges and rice cakes, Japanese frozen vegetables and rice, and teriyaki meatballs. Teachers read folktales like *Tikki Tikki Timbo* to the children and taught them how to say hello and good-bye in Japanese. At the end of the week, one of the teachers who had been to Japan brought in a kimono, doll, fish kite, tea set, and photographs for the children to see.

Questions

1. Which of the five approaches does this program use? Give three examples to back up your answer.

2. What are the strengths of this approach to multicultural education?

3. What are the weaknesses of this approach to multicultural education?

4. What might the long-term consequences be for a child who attends this program?

5. What would you add or eliminate from the multicultural education curriculum in this program?

Approaches to Multicultural Education

Case Study Three: Summit Children's Center

The children's program at Summit Children's Center is cognitively oriented. Teachers attempt to apply the theories of Jean Piaget to early childhood education. As a result, the learning experiences have a basis in developmental theory. Teachers try to be sensitive to the developmental needs and learning styles of each child. Emphasis is on the process of learning and growing rather than on learning facts and content. Teachers spend a great deal of time arranging classroom interest areas and rotating materials on a regular basis. Large blocks of free play insure that children are actively involved in their own learning. Brief large-group times foster social development and give teachers an opportunity to observe children's abilities or understanding.

Last year, the teaching staff realized that the children were noticing racial and cultural differences. One teacher overheard children making derogatory comments about Native Americans in picture books. Another teacher showed her class multi-ethnic photographs of children. Two Euro-American boys looked at a photo of an African American toddler watching his mother prepare to make breakfast. They thought the boy was going to steal the eggs.

The teaching staff met together and began going through the classroom's materials and bulletin boards. They wanted to make sure that people of color were adequately and positively represented in the classroom. They made posters and collages out of magazine pictures to show the diversity of people living in our country today. Next, staff made games and offered activities that gave children an opportunity to represent themselves, make connections between experiences, and correct distorted concepts or ideas. Skin color paints, crayons, and mirrors are now a permanent part of the art area. Multi-ethnic dolls and props are in the dramatic play area. Skin color, people and objects, faces, and hands and feet file folder games give children an opportunity to label, match, classify, and seriate.

Questions

1. Which of the five approaches does this program use? Give three examples to back up your answer.

2. What are the strengths of this approach to multicultural education?

3. What are the weaknesses of this approach to multicultural education?

4. What might the long-term consequences be for a child who attends this program?

5. What would you add or eliminate from the multicultural education curriculum in this program?

Approaches to Multicultural Education

Case Study Four: Community Child Care Center

Community Child Care is a neighborhood child care center with a history of extensive parent and community involvement. The center's mission is to provide quality care for all children. It mainstreams special needs children and has policies to ensure racial and economic diversity among the families and staff participating in the program.

The children's program is also structured to model and celebrate diversity. While the teachers utilize a traditional unit theme approach, they try to select "socially oriented" themes like families, friends, heroes, and workers. Staff carefully choose materials and create learning experiences that will foster age awareness, gender awareness, sex role identity, racial awareness, disability awareness, and cultural understanding.

Community Child Care seeks to instill a strong sense of personal and social responsibility in children. Staff try to model respect and use nonbiased language. Staff challenge children when they use biased language or make derogatory comments toward others. The classrooms are set up as mini-democracies, with the children actively participating in the decision-making.

Sometimes staff, parents, and children join together on a project. Last summer everyone was involved in painting the classrooms. Children helped choose the paint and actually participated alongside parents in painting the walls. The playground was rebuilt through a cooperative effort of staff, parents, and children. Children helped design the playground and were in charge of holding down wood while it was hammered, distributing sand, and testing equipment. When the need arises, the children are involved in helping to solve social problems. For example, motorists were driving above the speed limit down the center's street. This was a big concern during times of arrival and departure. The center does not have a parking lot. Parents park on the street to load and unload their children. The children and families made their own sign, requested a sign from the local public works department, wrote letters to the city council, and finally attended a city council meeting before receiving a sign that read, Caution When Children Present.

Questions

1. Which of the five approaches does this program use? Give three examples to back up your answer.

2. What are the strengths of this approach to multicultural education?

3. What are the weaknesses of this approach to multicultural education?

4. What might the long-term consequences be for a child who attends this program?

5. What would you add or eliminate from the multicultural education curriculum in this program?

Practical Application: Declaration of Acceptance and Goal Setting   **30 minutes**

Distribute a copy of the "Declaration of Acceptance" handout to each participant. Describe the importance of accepting a situation and setting goals prior to taking action. Tell participants to write brief paragraphs describing why they believe multicultural education is important and an appropriate focus for an early childhood teacher.

Next, ask participants to write their own goals for multicultural education. "A GOAL is a statement or declaration of an intentional result or outcome…it doesn't tell you how to get there but merely where you want to end up…tomorrow, next month, five years from now, decades from now" (Koberg and Bagnall, 1981, 108).

Complete the activity by asking students to sign and date their declaration of acceptance and goals and to find a witness to sign and date the declaration.

Adapted from Don Koberg and Jim Bagnall, *The Revised All New Universal Traveler.* Los Altos, CA: William Kaufman, Inc., 1981.

Declaration of Acceptance

I declare that _____

_____

_____

_____

_____

As a result, I set these goals for multicultural education

1. _____
   _____

2. _____
   _____

3. _____
   _____

4. _____
   _____

5. _____
   _____

6. _____
   _____

7. _____
   _____

8. _____
   _____

9. _____
   _____

10. _____
    _____

Signed_____date_____

Witnessed by_____date_____

Journaling

1. Which of the five approaches to multicultural education fits with your beliefs? Why?
2. Which of the five approaches best matches what is currently taking place in your classroom? Give three examples.

Affirmations

Symbol: key

1. I recognize the importance of culture in children's lives.
2. I teach children about their own culture.
3. I respect other cultures.
4. I create a learning/caregiving environment where everyone is welcome.
5. I help children to like themselves.
6. I am entitled to my cultural heritage.
7. I am proud of my cultural heritage.
8. I prepare children to live in a multicultural society.
9. I introduce children to other cultures.
10. I choose an approach to multicultural education.
11. I avoid tourist activities that stereotype people.
12. I challenge myself by setting goals for multicultural education.

Additional Activities

Panel Discussion

Organize a panel of teachers or directors from local early childhood programs that implement some form of multicultural education. Before the panel members arrive, have the class participants brainstorm questions to ask the panel. Give each of them time to present their approach, goals, and types of activities they use to implement their curriculum. Follow up with class participants taking turns asking the prepared questions. After the panel members leave facilitate a large group discussion. Consider asking participants to identify the strengths, weaknesses, and their personal preferences.

The Cultural Diversity Debate

There are differing opinions as to whether or not multicultural education is necessary and beneficial. Help students put these arguments into perspective by giving them an opportunity to debate the issues. Inform the class that there will be two debates. In the first debate two groups will present their positions related to the need for and importance of multicultural education. One group will take the position that multicultural education is a necessity. The opposing group will take the position that multicultural education is an elective or a luxury.

In the second debate two groups will discuss whether diversity gives us strength and wholeness or diversity divides us and makes us weaker. One small group will take the position that diversity makes society stronger and the other small group will argue that diversity tears apart a society.

Ask participants to choose which debate and which position they would like to take. Once the small groups have been established, give them time to form their arguments, rebuttals, and closing remarks. Encourage them to strategize how to present their group's position. Remind participants that everyone needs to be involved in the debate.

Call the class together. Tell them you will moderate the debate. The other half of the class that is not participating will be the audience/judges and they will decide which group made the best case for their position. One way to organize a debate is to give each side five minutes to present their case, two minutes of rebuttal, five more minutes to further state their case, two minutes of rebuttal, and two minutes of closing argument.

Remind participants to think of this as a role play. They may not personally agree with the position they are presenting and defending. But it is important to fully take on that perspective for the duration of the exercise.

Letter to the Editor

This activity will help participants think through and articulate a response to parents and co-workers who think that there is too much emphasis on culture, race, and people of color in education. Say:

This letter to the editor recently appeared in your local paper.

Dear Editor:

I am thoroughly disgusted with all of the coverage you have given to this multi-cultural stuff. All I ever read about is African Americans, Native Americans, Hispanic Americans, Asian Americans. What is happening? Are these folks trying to destroy our country? America is a melting pot nation. Our forefathers were willing to leave the old country behind, set aside their differences, and band together to create this wonderful nation of ours.

Our hope for the future is with the future, not the past. If America is going to continue to be the great nation that she is then people are going to have to start calling themselves Americans and show their pride in America. If we don't stop this multicultural trend we won't have any Americans left.

If people want to immigrate here and take advantage of the opportunity for a better life—fine. I am willing to share. But they'd better be willing to learn English, become American citizens, and act like Americans.

I say America: love it or leave it,

Proud American

Your director is concerned that perhaps some of the parents and staff at your program share this person's attitudes. She knows you are interested in multicultural education and asks you to write an article for the parent newsletter responding to these issues.

Beginning with Me: Racial Awareness for Teachers

Description

Multicultural education begins with us, the teachers. Prepare for multicultural education by affirming our racial identity and examining racism and prejudice in our lives. Gain new understanding of what you can do to promote cultural acceptance and respect. (**Note:** This session is based on Carol Morgaine's model of self-formation. You may want to refer to pages 40-42 of *Roots and Wings* in preparation for this session and ask participants to read these pages as a follow-up to this session. In addition, it takes at least four hours to go through the material. Plan an extended session or devote two back-to-back sessions.)

Goals

1. Identify oneself in terms of color, race, and culture.
2. Associate power with racism.
3. Recognize own defenses against racial awareness.
4. Apply racism to institutions.
5. Recognize Euro-American's responsibility for racism.
6. Compare attitude to actions.

Ice Breaker: Identify Yourself   25 minutes

As participants arrive, ask them to form small groups and begin discussing the following questions:

1. How do you describe yourself in terms of skin color, race, and culture?
2. What do you like about being part of your racial or cultural group?
3. What is difficult about being part of your racial or cultural group?
4. What does your racial or cultural group stand for?
5. What does it mean to be a person of your race or culture?

You may want to make a handout of the questions. This will allow participants to jot down their answers and refer to the questions throughout their discussion. If the class is racially mixed, consider asking the people of color to form their own group. This is for their own safety, so that they are not overwhelmed by having to listen to Euro-American's racism and are not forced into a position of speaking on behalf of their entire race or teaching the Euro-Americans about other races. Some Euro-Americans may have difficulty answering the questions, as it is their first experience in being asked to identify themselves racially. Don't accept "I don't know" for an answer. Gently prod them to identify what their race stands for. If they say,"I'm white. I'm American. I don't know what that means," ask them, "What does America stand for? What are America's values?" Make sure that participants have an understanding of white culture before moving on to the next exercises.

Problem Posing: What Is Power? How Does It Relate to Prejudice?   45 minutes

Large Group Discussion

Bring the group together and ask them to identify different cultural groups represented in their small group. List all the groups on the chalkboard. If the list is very small, ask participants to name all of the cultural groups in their community or state. Make a transition to the next topic by saying:

Interpersonal dynamics are at play when two or more people, or two or more groups attempt to relate to one another. In a family people try to live together. At work people try to get a job done. In a society people try to live side-by-side in harmony. One of the dynamics that is an important part of multiracial or multicultural relationships is power.

Lead a group discussion on power. Ask: What is power? Who has power in our society? Who doesn't have power in our society? What are the characteristics of people with power in our society? How do they use power to control those without power? How does power relate to prejudice?

Introduce the concept that racism is "prejudice plus power." According to this definition, racial minorities cannot be racist against those who hold the power in this county. Racial minorities "…may be prejudiced against whites, but clearly they do not have the power to enforce that prejudice" (Katz, 1978, 50).

Body Sculpting

This is a technique originally developed by Virginia Satir. Body sculpting gives participants an opportunity to gain new understanding to the effects of racism in our lives. Divide the class into small groups of three to four participants. Each person takes a turn "sculpting" how they experience racism. The sculptor plays herself, assigns roles to the other small group members, and positions them to create the body sculpture. The sculptor joins the sculpture and the group holds the position for one minute. Afterwards, the sculptor and group members take turns talking about how it felt to be in that position. Next, the sculptor creates a new sculpture of how she would like to experience race relations. Again hold the position for one minute. Only this time the sculptor talks about how it feels to be in that position while still in the position. Continue until each person in the small group has a turn to create two sculptures. End the exercise by discussing how racism affects our lives.

Presentation of Content: Shame and the Development of Racial Awareness   30 minutes

Mini-Lecture: A Developmental Perspective on Racial Awareness

Say to your students:

You may be asking yourself: "Am I prejudiced? Am I racist? If so, how did I get that way?" As young children we're busy developing our sense of self. Self-concept includes racial or cultural identity.

One way to figure out who you are is to compare yourself with others. Infants and toddlers do this all the time. They are always trying to figure out what's me and what's not me. Chances are once you acquired language and moved into the pre-operational stage, you were filled with an "insatiable curiosity." In an attempt to clarify your own self-concept, answer your curiosity, and clarify any distorted thoughts you asked questions and blurted out ideas. You know, things like "I don't like black people." "Why he so muddy?" " Look at that funny lady." "Not him, I mean the black one." "Dat not a man, dat a bear."

Parents and adults, being the dominant member in adult-child relationships, often respond to these remarks in powerful ways. Through their response, parents attempt to control their child's behavior, thoughts, or feelings. They want you to stop now. Unfortunately the response often received is one of shaming. The parent uses power to shame, humiliate, or embarrass the child. The child feels exposed, defective, stupid, and becomes silent. The child's thinking is likely, "Wow, I must really be bad. Something must be wrong with me because I can't help noticing those differences, and nobody else sees them. Here are some examples of shaming adult responses:

When the child says, "I don't like black people." The adult responds, "Oh yes you do. I don't want to hear you say that ever again."

When the child asks, "Why is he so muddy?" The adult answers, "I don't know, it doesn't matter. We are all the same."

When the child says, " Look at that funny lady." The parent responds by tensing up, grabbing the child's hand tightly, pulling her close, and walking quickly away. When they get to the car the parent says, "Do you know how much you embarrassed me in the store today?"

When the child says, "Dat not a man, dat a bear." The adult responds, "Where did you get that stupid idea? Stop that nonsense this instant."

When the child stares at a person of color. The parent responds, "Stop it. It's not nice to stare."

Another shame response is to cover or hide one's face. When children are shamed for noticing racial differences or wonder about race, they learn to cover their eyes and they stop noticing the differences. It's self-protection. They found out it kept them from getting into trouble. Instead of developing a healthy racial identity, racial awareness, and positive racial attitudes, children learn to deny their racial identity and awareness to prevent being shamed and humiliated by the powerful adults in their lives.

Shame becomes internalized. This means that a part of yourself takes on the identity of the shamer. This part of ourselves is called the critical parent. Some people experience internalized shame in the form of a voice that says things like: "I told you so." "You are so stupid." "See, you can't ever do anything right." Others experience shame as a feeling or sensation such as a funny feeling in their stomach. You might find that as an adult you get these feelings or thoughts when you think about noticing someone's skin color, race, or culture. You may think it is bad to notice differences because of your early experience. In this way you may be shaming yourself and therefore keeping yourself at a very early stage of racial awareness.

Small Group Discussion

Divide the class into small groups and ask them to discuss the following questions:

1. What are some additional examples of how adults commonly respond in a shaming manner to children's racial curiosity or racial comments?
2. As a child what were you taught about your own racial identity?
3. As a child what were you taught about other races?
4. How and what were you taught about racial groups?

Distribute the handout "Stages of Racial Awareness." Ask participants to read the handout and identify which stage they are at. Next, ask them to identify at which stage they would like to be in their development of racial awareness. You might also ask participants to review the list of stereotypes commonly accepted by young children on page 171 in *Roots and Wings*. Ask them: "What stereotypes from your childhood still haunt you?"

Critical Reflection: Defenses Against
Racial Awareness   **30 minutes**

Introduce the concept of defenses as a hindrance to racial awareness. Say:

Naturally, we want to protect ourselves from feelings of shame. Defenses are one type of psychological protection. Defenses are different forms of distorted thinking. When the truth is painful, defenses work to deny that truth and create a false reality. Defenses are very prevalent among Euro-Americans when it comes to racial awareness. Defenses have been used to create the illusion that America is a color-blind society.

Distribute the handout "Defenses Against Racial Awareness." Briefly review each of the defenses with the class. Ask participants to generate examples of each of the defenses, identify which defenses they use, and to add any defenses they may think of. Below are some typical responses:

1. All African Americans are drug dealers.
2. All Hispanics are dirty.
3. She'll like rice—she's Japanese. He'll love music time because he's African American.
4. We're all the same. Culture isn't important, it doesn't really matter. We don't have those problems here.
5. They have to learn the ways of our culture sooner or later.
6. Providers say their slots are filled when they do have openings.
7. What will the neighbors think? I think the other parents will pull their kids out of my program if I take the black child.
8. Children are too young to notice differences.
9. That's a spoiled baby—that mother holds the baby too much. They should move back to their own neighborhood.
10. I have to meet the needs of the whole group. We don't have money for new materials.

Defenses Against Racial Awareness

1. Filtering. Focus on one negative aspect and ignore all the the positive aspects of a person or a racial group.

   _____
   _____
   _____

2. Overgeneralization. Generalized thinking based on a single experience or one piece of information.

   _____
   _____
   _____

3. Mind reading. Make assumptions or judgments about a person without knowing or having proof.

   _____
   _____
   _____

4. Denial. Reality is treated as though it does not exist.

   _____
   _____
   _____

5. Rationalization. Convince ourselves that we have not acted in a way that conflicts with our standards.

   _____
   _____
   _____

6. Withdrawal. Avoid or flee from threatening situations, becoming fearful of racial diversity and people who are different.

   _____
   _____
   _____

7. Catastrophizing. Expect and imagine the worst disaster. "What if…" thinking.

   _____
   _____
   _____

8. Minimizing. Disguise differences by reducing or discounting them.

   _____
   _____
   _____

9. Blaming. Other people are responsible or the cause of problems.

   _____
   _____
   _____

10. Helplessness. Innocent because the situation is out of your control, nothing can be done about it.

   _____
   _____
   _____

Adapted from McKay, Matthew, Martha Davis, and Patrick Fanning, *Thoughts & Feelings: The Art of Cognitive Stress Intervention.* Richmond, CA: New Harbinger Publications, 1981.

Practical Application: Identifying and Eliminating Racism   105 minutes

Say to your class:

The defenses we've identified are not just characteristics of individual behavior. They are also part of the dynamics of systems like families, day care centers, school, social service agencies, governments, and entire societies. Some examples of the distorted thinking that influences how a group operates are:

> *Control: Bad things will happen if Euro-Americans aren't in control.*

> *Dualistic Thinking: Euro-Americans are good, superior and other cultures are bad, inferior.*

> *Blame: Euro-Americans are not to blame for society's problems. It is the fault of the minorities.*

> *Unreliable: You can't trust or rely on people of other races or cultures. Only trust yourself and people just like you.*

> *No-Talk Rule: Don't talk about or notice cultural diversity, racial differences, or prejudice. Deny that it exists.*

> *Zero-Sum: There isn't enough to go around.*

> *Non-Participatory: People are the objects (rather than subjects) of a system that doesn't change.*

> *Promote Dishonesty: It is difficult for individuals to be honest with themselves and function within the system.*

Adapted from Carol Morgaine, *Process Parenting: Breaking the Addictive Cycle*. St. Paul: Minnesota Department of Human Services, 1988.

A Racist Community

This activity helps participants understand that oppression is institutionalized racism. Divide the class into small groups of four to five participants. Give each group a piece of chart paper and some felt tip markers or crayons. Tell them to design a racist community. They can use words or draw a picture. The community must must be detailed and include: population and racial make up; the decision makers; the decision making process; who controls the money; who sets the policies; the role of child care, schools, churches, business, media, social organizations, and recreational centers. Give the groups thirty minutes to create their communities. Bring everyone together and ask the small groups to take turns describing their community. After all of the racist communities have been presented, facilitate a discussion around these questions:

> What makes a community racist?

> How is your community like real cities in America? How is it different?

> Who has the power to oppress?

Adapted from Judith Katz, *White Awareness*. Norman, OK: University of Oklahoma Press, 1978.

Guided Imagery

Tell participants that it is critical they recognize the role of society and institution in the perpetuation of racism. As this class draws to a close, you want them to focus back on themselves. This guided imagery will help them reflect on the concepts presented today. Say:

Find a comfortable position. Relax your arms allowing your hands to rest in your lap. Close your eyes and breathe deeply. As you breathe feel your body relax.

*

Return to your authentic self. Perhaps you are an infant, a toddler, or a preschooler. Return to a time when you were in touch with your true self and freely expressed yourself. Find that authenticity in yourself today. Experience your goodness, your uniqueness, and curiosity. Acknowledge and affirm your true self as the source of your identity, integrity, and strength.

*

Return to a time when you first experienced your power. What is the source of your power? Is it knowing who you are and being attuned to yourself? Every human being has power. Claim the power that is rightfully yours. Use your power to give expression and voice to your true self.

*

You are an adult now. Use you power as an adult to protect yourself from shame and self judgement. Invite the voice of your true self to replace the nagging, critical voice inside your head. Next, imagine that your power is like a new skin that protects you from the hurtful words and actions of others. You decide when to be vulnerable and when to shield yourself in protection.

*

As a child, you built up walls around you because you were powerless in a shaming world. What are your protective walls made of? Denial? Minimizing? Blaming? Ignoring? Rationalizing? Recognize how these responses separate you from the rest of humanity. Imagine those walls coming down, crumbling to the ground. Know that your adult power and authentic voice will keep you safe. Trust in the goodness of others, others who are racially or culturally different from you.

*

Return to your family of origin. Notice how you learned to relate to others through addictive patterns. What did you learn about control? Perhaps there was one dominating, controlling person or everything felt out of control. What role did perfection play in your family? Did you have to be perfect in order to be accepted? Was one person always right and the other person wrong? What style of communication did you learn from your family? Did people talk openly and honestly or were there "no talk" rules about certain topics? Recognize how these patterns grew out of your shame and defenses against shame. Take these patterns one-by-one and release them from your body, transforming the destructive patterns into positive ones. Cleanse yourself from the past. Feel your true self and your positive adult power.

*

Notice your current life. How have the defenses and negative patterns of interaction been used to keep you isolated, segregated? In what ways have you ignored, degraded, defined, dismissed, doubted, distrusted, or blamed people because of their race or culture? How have you operated out of assumptions and stereotypes? This is negativity inherited from the past. You did not ask for it, but now you must be responsible for your prejudiced thinking and behavior. Prejudice keeps you and others from being fully human. Take your prejudice and transform it. Fill yourself with love, peace, gentleness, kindness, openness, and security. Remember and embrace your authentic self which is full of goodness.

*

Recognize all of the ways in which society does not respect and honor human beings. Acknowledge how the structures, the institutions perpetuate prejudice. The result is dehumanizing, and you feel it deep within you. Feel the powerlessness of an individual trying to change a system. Now transform your powerlessness and hopelessness into outrage. Your awareness creates a righteous anger. Use this energy to envision a new society where all people are valued. Imagine yourself working with others, collectively, to create a new society that is respectful, safe, and humane. Know that if you can imagine it, you can create it.

Journaling

Write the following quote on the chalkboard: "We have met the enemy and they are us." Ask participants to write their answers to these questions.

1. How does this saying relate to racism?
2. Who is responsible for racism and racial inequality?
3. What can you do to eliminate racism in your life?

Affirmations

Symbol: butterfly

Affirmations are a way of replacing the critical self-talk and the voice of hopelessness with truth, acceptance, and personal responsibility. Print the butterfly shape on card stock. Give participants scissors and two or three sheets of the butterflies. List the affirmations so that everyone can read them. Ask participants to make their own affirmation cards by writing an affirmation inside each butterfly and cutting out the shapes. They can copy the affirmations on the chalkboard or write their own. Perhaps a new awareness came to them in the guided imagery, and they would like to write an affirmation about it.

1. I affirm my racial identity.
2. I affirm my cultural identity.
3. I take responsibility for my racial attitudes.
4. I seek greater racial awareness and understanding.
5. I establish and maintain respectful relationships with people outside of my culture.
6. As a member of the dominant culture, I release my feelings of guilt and helplessness.

7. I challenge racism in my life.
8. I challenge racism on my job.
9. I challenge racism in my community.
10. I am a powerful person.
11. My attitudes and actions make a difference.
12. I eliminate defenses that distort the truth.

Additional Activities

Symbolize Your Empowerment Process

Symbols are very important to me. They serve as reminders and commemorate important events in my life. I bought a print on my thirtieth birthday. My twenties had been rather tumultuous and I wanted to celebrate and commemorate the fact that I was entering a new decade. Another time I used a symbol to help me tackle a large project when I was writing my master's thesis. I had short hair and decided to grow a ponytail at the nape of my neck. I kept my hair short, except for the ponytail, for the next two years while I researched and wrote the thesis. It was a symbol and constant reminder of the commitment I made to myself to complete my education.

Encourage participants to find a symbol for themselves to commemorate their personal growth. It can be anything meaningful to the participant. The important thing is that the individual identifies with the symbol. I've had participants bring in a rose bush, a rock, a photograph, a necklace. Talk about the importance of symbols.

Ask participants to be on the lookout for something that symbolizes their racial awareness, goals for multicultural education, and commitment to ending racism. Remind them that the symbol doesn't have to be bought. It can be something from nature, something found, or something handmade. They will know it when they see it. Ask them to bring it to the last night of class and share it with the rest of the group.

Interview

Interview an elderly person who shares your cultural heritage. If you are Euro-American, try to find someone who immigrated from the same country as your ancestors. What are the truths of your culture? Cultural truth is based on human experience and is not static. It is always changing. How have this person's thoughts and feelings about his culture changed over the years? How did being a _____ person help you become an American? How did being a _____ person make it difficult for you to become an American? What is your cultural truth? What does it mean to you to be a _____ person? How might your attitude toward your own cultural identity influence how you view other people's cultural identity?

Identifying Racism

Ask participants to bring something to class that represents racism. It could be a picture, object, newspaper article, song, poem, greeting card, poster, piece of clothing, or advertisement. Divide the class into small groups. Give each group a piece of chart paper and a felt tip marker. Ask them to choose a recorder. Have each participant share the object with the small group and identify why it seems racist. Pass the object around and give each person an opportunity to respond to it by answering these questions: Can you identify with the object? How does it represent racism? How doesn't it represent racism?

Once all of the objects have been shared, ask the group to make a list of what is and isn't racist. Next, review the list and identify the contradictions, if there are any. Finish the activity by asking the groups to discuss this question: As a result of analyzing the objects, what do you know about the forces behind racism?

Write a Position Statement on Multicultural Education

This activity helps participants make the transition from examining personal attitudes to taking informed action. Most adults have strongly held beliefs about children, how they learn, what they should learn, and what would make America an ideal society.

Tell participants to write out their position on multicultural education. Address these issues:

Authenticity of children	Who are they? What are their characteristics? Are they basically good or bad? Are they active or passive learners?
Power	What is power? How do children experience power? What do you want to teach them about power? How will you teach them?
Shame	How is children's authenticity oppressed? When and how do children experience humiliation?
Defenses	How can you teach children to protect themselves from shame? How can you reduce children's need to use denial, minimizing, isolation, or blaming as a defense against diversity?
Addictive Systems	How do early childhood programs discourage authenticity in children? How can you help children establish and maintain healthy relationships?
Prejudice	How do -isms affect your program? How can you help children develop positive racial attitudes?
Oppression	How does your program oppress children or families? How can you challenge hopelessness and empower children to take action against oppression?

Review your theoretical statement by asking yourself these questions:

    Does it match or express my personal experience?
    Does it make sense to me?
    Is it comprehensive?
    Does it give me a sense of direction?

Creating a Definition of Prejudice

Ask participants to write their own definition of prejudice on a piece of paper. Have them form a small group with two or three others. Tell them to read their definitions to one another and create a group definition that incorporates the individual definitions. Ask each of the small groups to share their definition with the large group. Definitions could be written on sheets of newsprint and posted around the classroom for all to see. Discuss the similarities and differences among the definitions. What seem to be the important elements? Read the definition of prejudice from a dictionary to the class. Compare the dictionary definition to the definitions that the participants wrote.

I Dream a World

Ask participants to take a moment to reflect on their vision for the world. Ask: "What is your dream for the world?" and "What kind of place would you like the world to be?" Tell participants to draw or write their dream for the world. When they finish, ask them to form small groups and present their visions for the world with each other. Ask the groups to identify: What dreams are shared among yourselves? In what areas are we closest to achieving the dream? What areas need the most work to achieve the dream?

Finish the activity by having the groups write or draw a shared dream.

At the Movies

Assign participants to watch a current movie or home video that relates to racial awareness, prejudice, and oppression. Participants can brainstorm a list of movie titles. Say:

Choose one film from the list generated during class. Watch the movie and analyze it for authenticity, power, shame, defenses, and racist systems. Write a review of the film, answering these questions.

1. *What was the film's title?*

2. *What was the film about? Briefly describe the film.*

3. *Who was the main character?*

4. *Who was this person?*

5. *How was power used on this person? How did this person use power?*

6. *How did this person experience shame related to race or culture?*

7. *What was this person ashamed of? Who shamed this person?*

8. *What defenses did the character use in response?*

9. *What systems was the character involved in?*

10. *What characteristics of a racist system did you observe?*

11. *How did the racism inherent in the system oppress the character?*

12. *What was the character's response?*

Culture Sharing

Ask participants to come to the class session prepared to share something about their culture. They might choose to share some information about their culture, tell a family story that relates to their culture, or bring an object. Once everyone has arrived, invite each participant to take a turn sharing her culture.

Guided Imagery: Receiving Our Ancestors

Tell your class they will now do a guided imagery. Say:

Focus your attention on your heart. Your heart has healing forces. Ask your heart to transform you. Imagine a rainbow of colors pouring out of your heart to bring peace and harmony to the world. Let the rainbow of healing power from your heart heal you and protect you.

*

Imagine yourself traveling back to when your ancestors lived in their native homeland. Where did they live? What were they doing? What did they look like? How did they care for their children? Watch closely. Notice and remember the details.

*

Ask one of your ancestors to come and talk with you. You have three minutes of clock time, which is all the time you will need. Ask your ancestor to tell you what is true for your people. What part of your culture has been lost? How can you understand and affirm your culture? What do you need to respect other cultures? What can you do to promote racial harmony?

*

Now it's time to say good-bye to your ancestor. Look around and notice the details before you go. Thank your ancestor for joining you and say good-bye. Return to the present time and your body. Feel yourself sitting in this room. When you are ready open your eyes.

The Do's and Taboos of Implementing Multicultural Education

Description

Get on track and stay there by following the seven steps toward implementing multicultural education. Learn how to get the entire staff involved in multicultural education and recognize the common pitfalls that can prevent a program from successfully achieving its goals.

Goals

1. Recognize the complexity of implementing multicultural education.
2. Examine the seven steps to implementing multicultural education.
3. Identify staff responsibilities in implementing multicultural education.
4. Develop a plan for implementing multicultural education at your site.

Ice Breaker: Where Do We Start?   20 minutes

As participants arrive, ask them to find a partner and make a list of their questions about implementing multicultural education. After about five minutes bring the class together. Ask one pair to share their questions. Write the questions on the chalkboard. Next, ask the second pair to state any questions they have that are different from the ones already listed. Add these to the list on the chalkboard. Continue in this manner until all the pairs have contributed their questions about implementing multicultural education.

Review the list with the class and acknowledge the complexity of implementing multicultural education. You might want to spend a few minutes answering some of the questions.

Problem Posing: Understand The Process   15 minutes

Large Group Discussion

Pose the question: "If multicultural education is this complex, how can we insure success in implementing multicultural education?" In other words, how can we avoid getting stuck? Discuss tactics for insuring success. Include suggestions such as allow plenty of time, start where you are, change "things" first, find support, talk about what you are doing, and expect to make mistakes. You may want to refer to pages 32-34 in *Roots and Wings* for additional information.

Checklist

Distribute a copy of the handout "What's Your Excuse?" This checklist will help participants recognize and reflect on the elements that hold them back from implementing multicultural education.

What's My Excuse?

Many teachers are totally overwhelmed by the notion of implementing multicultural education. Others are closed to the possibilities. Sometimes we have to explore what is holding us back before we can move ahead. Ask yourself: What's my excuse? What is holding me back?

_____lack of knowledge

_____fear

_____indifference

_____prejudice

_____too tired

_____overwhelmed

_____hate change

_____lack of time

_____lack of support

_____don't want to be the only one

_____not interested

_____like things the way they are

_____lack materials

_____don't want to commit

_____lack of desire

_____don't want a challenge

_____other priorities

_____don't value it

_____don't want to rock the boat

_____don't want to be seen as a radical

_____other things are more important

_____multicultural education isn't relevant to my community

How can you eliminate your excuses?

Presentation of Content: Implementing Multicultural Education   45 minutes

Mini-Lecture: Steps to Implementing Multicultural Education in the Classroom

Present the seven steps to implementing multicultural education in the classroom. Refer to pages 42-46 in *Roots and Wings*. Make a handout or an overhead of the steps.

Brainstorm: Integrating Multicultural Education into the Entire Program

Tape four sheets of chart paper to the wall. Label them administrators, support the staff, cooks, and parents. As a large group, brainstorm how each group influences multicultural education, and their roles and responsibilities in implementing multicultural education.

Critical Reflection: What Can You Do on Behalf of Multicultural Education?   15 minutes

Distribute the checklist "What Can I Do on Behalf of Multicultural Education?" Ask participants to check those actions they are willing to take. Next, ask them to draw a line through the action they are definitely not willing to take. Then ask them to prioritize the remaining actions in the order which they are willing to complete the tasks. Ask participants to share the results with someone else in the room.

What Can I Do on Behalf of Multicultural Education?

Check which actions you are willing to take on behalf of multicultural education. Draw a line through the actions you would definitely not take. Go through the list a second time and rank the actions in the order you are willing to take, with one being the first thing you will do.

_____ 1. Write an article for a parent newsletter.

_____ 2. Take a class or attend a workshop on multicultural education.

_____ 3. Read a book on multicultural education.

_____ 4. Visit an early childhood program that is implementing multicultural education.

_____ 5. Learn about another culture.

_____ 6. Examine your own racial attitudes and assumptions.

_____ 7. Join a teacher/director support group.

_____ 8. Write a letter to a toy company calling their attention to stereotypic toys and games.

_____ 9. Ask your local bookseller or librarian to stock more multicultural children's books.

_____ 10. Attend a community event sponsored by an ethnic group other than your own.

_____ 11. Evaluate the children's books in your program.

_____ 12. Make a multicultural game or learning activity.

_____ 13. Ask your director to purchase multicultural materials for your program.

_____ 14. Revise a curriculum unit to incorporate multicultural goals and concepts.

_____ 15. Challenge a child's discriminatory behavior.

_____ 16. Organize a cultural diversity or inclusiveness committee at your program.

_____ 17. Organize a multicultural education inservice workshop for the staff at your program.

_____ 18. Share information on multicultural education with your co-workers.

_____ 19. Refuse to celebrate holidays that promote stereotypes.

_____ 20. Invite a parent to come into your classroom and share his culture.

_____ 21. Write a grant to fund the multicultural curriculum project at your program.

_____ 22. Start a parent education group to explore cultural awareness and attitudes in children.

_____ 23. Testify on behalf of multicultural education at your state legislature.

_____ 24. Conduct a multicultural workshop.

_____ 25. Write your own:

_____

_____

_____

Practical Application: Envisioning Multicultural Education in Our Program   60 minutes

Guided Imagery: Multicultural Action Shield

Implementing multicultural education requires reflective action, that is, action that results from personal reflection and critical analysis. To be successful in implementing multicultural education in our programs, staff must thoroughly assess their situation. Tell them:

We will make action shields to illustrate our individual paths to implementing multicultural education. Many cultures use shields or crests to describe themselves. Today we will make shields that will be divided into six sections: our skills, the current situation, forces hindering, forces assisting, dream for the future, and action steps to achieve our vision. After the guided imagery, you will be given paper and art materials for making a shield.

*

Make yourself comfortable and close your eyes. Take three slow, deep breaths, letting go of tension as you exhale. Focus your attention on your forehead. Imagine a dot between your eyes. As you focus on the dot, it gets warmer and warmer. Like the sun that warms you, it radiates its energy outward. It grows and grows until its circle of warmth encompasses you.

*

It is safe and warm inside this circle. Take some time to notice the skills and talents you bring to multicultural education. These talents give you confidence and help you feel good about yourself.

*

Notice the current role of multicultural education in your program. How is multicultural education incorporated into the total program? Who is involved?

*

Notice the forces that will help your program add or improve multicultural education. Are they large or small positive forces? Perhaps there are people that can help or resources available.

*

Notice the forces that are preventing or hindering the addition or improvement of multicultural education in your program. Are they large or small negative forces? Perhaps personal fear and anxiety, ignorance, or lack of resources are hindering you.

*

Now take time to create a vision for the future of multicultural education in your program.

*

How will you make your dream come true? What action steps do you and your co-workers need to take to successfully implement multicultural education in your program?

*

Prepare to join me in this room and make an action shield that represents your imagination. When you are ready open your eyes and join me in this room.

Adapted from Maureen Murdock, the Peace Shield Activity in *Spinning Inward*, Boston: Shambhala Publications, Inc., 1987.

Making a Multicultural Action Shield

Give each participant a piece of chart paper or oak tag. Set out felt tip markers and crayons. Write on the chalkboard the six items that should be included in the shield. You can substitute the form "Envisioning Multicultural Education in Our Program" on page 36 of *Roots and Wings* for the shield.

Bring the class back together when participants are done (approximately 30 minutes) and ask each participant to share her shield with the rest of the class.

Journaling

1. What information would you like and what skills do you need to develop in order to implement a multicultural curriculum?
2. As a teacher, how might you need to change in order to effectively implement multicultural education?
3. With whom can you share this project? Who will support you?

Affirmations

Symbol: shield

1. I trust the process of implementing multicultural education.
2. I release the excuses that hold me back.
3. I face my resistance to change.
4. I live with the complexity of multicultural education.
5. I am patient with myself.
6. I start today where I am.
7. I set goals for myself.
8. I seek support for my work from others.
9. I willingly work with others to implement multicultural education.
10. I give myself permission to make mistakes.
11. I visualize my dream for multicultural education.
12. I am open to change.

Additional Activities

Name the Project

Naming the project is another way to promote multicultural education within a program. Naming is an act of personalizing; it makes the project our own. When we name a project ourselves, we are more likely to identify with it and be committed to it. Naming is also important because it is likely that what we call multicultural education affects the kind of curriculum we create. Here are some examples of names staff have given to multicultural projects.

Read the following names of multicultural curriculum projects. What do you think of when you see these names? For each name, write down your answer to the following questions: What might be the purpose of such a curriculum project? What types of activities might they use to achieve their goals?

Project Name	Purpose	Activities
Global Classroom		
Rainbow Curriculum		
Multicultural Education		
Cultural Diversity		
Anti-Bias		
World Citizenship		
Let Me Be Me		
Cultural Awareness		
Building Bridges		
Children Around the World		

Symbolize the Project

Another way to personalize and promote a multicultural curriculum project is to symbolize it. A local elementary school is beginning the second year of a multicultural, gender-fair, and disability-aware curriculum project. The name of the project is "Schools of Many Voices," and a large banner covers the foyer, proudly announcing that this is the district demonstration site. The first time I was in the building, I didn't know anything about the project but I noticed and remembered the banner. So that when a friend asked if I knew about the "Schools of Many Voices" project, my first response was "No, tell me about it." As I listened to a brief description of the project, I remembered the banner. I thought to myself, "Oh, that's what the banner was about." Visual images are a way of keeping a project in the forefront of our minds, and they force us to go "public" with our ideas, both of which work to keep the project alive.

There are at least three ways to symbolize a multicultural curriculum project. Posters, banners, and T-shirts can be used as promotion tools.

Posters. Set out pencils, felt tip markers, crayons, paints, construction paper, glue, and poster board. Divide the group into small groups and have each group design a poster that symbolizes the group's commonalties and the message being expressed through multicultural curriculum. Have staff from each classroom work together if you are providing inservice training to the staff of one program. Ask each small group to share their finished poster with the large group. One final poster could be designed by incorporating elements from each of the posters. Display the posters in the classroom or hallways along with a brief written description of the activity.

Banners. Banners are usually made from fabric and hang from the ceiling or on a wall. Have the group discuss the purpose of a banner and identify important elements to include in the design. Remember, it should be an expression of the groups commonalties and goals. Provide paper, pencils, and crayons so that participants can make preliminary sketches. People can work together as a large group or in small groups. Select a design and method. Some simple methods are: cutting out felt shapes and gluing them onto a felt or burlap background, coloring the design with fabric crayons on a piece of cotton fabric, painting the design with fabric paints on a piece of heavy cotton fabric. Ask for a volunteer to finish the edges with a sewing machine and prepare the banner for hanging.

T-Shirts/Sweat Shirts. T-shirts can be simple or elaborate. Each person can make their own by using fabric crayons or fabric paints on a plain cotton T-shirt. Staff can create a design using the process described above. Another option is to have T-shirts or sweat shirts printed professionally. You could have a design contest and invite both children and adults to submit entries. The designs would need to be "camera ready" in black ink on white paper. The winner would receive a free T-shirt or sweat shirt. T-shirts/sweat shirts could be sold to staff, parents, and children. The project could become a fund raiser if you can find an inexpensive local printer.

Rights and Responsibilities

Another way to identify multicultural goals and staff roles is to identify children's rights and adult responsibilities. Ask yourself: "What are the child's rights who attends our program?" "What is my responsibility as a teacher?" Study the handouts from "Clearwater Children's Center"; then write a child's bill of rights and a list of adult responsibilities for your program.

A Child's Bill of Rights at
Clearwater Children's Center

A child attending our program has the right to...

respect.

be recognized as a human being who is a family member and member of a culture.

high self-esteem and a positive self-concept.

learn about one's own culture.

learn about other cultures.

a relationship with consistent caregivers.

play with other children.

be curious.

feel good about oneself.

positive learning experiences without fear of failure.

discover the world.

laugh and be silly.

express oneself in many ways.

accurate information.

say "no."

a safe and healthy environment.

learn how to be a group member.

protection from physical and emotional harm.

Adult Responsibilities at
Clearwater Children's Center

We the teachers do solemnly vow to…

be aware of one's own prejudice attitudes.

be able to identify one's own culture.

demonstrate respect to all children and families.

provide culturally responsive child care.

match educational experiences with the children's social context.

set up and maintain a multicultural, gender-fair environment.

respond to children's biased remarks.

create and maintain a democratic classroom.

plan and implement developmentally appropriate multicultural activities.

A Child's Bill of Rights at

A child attending our program has the right to…

Adult Responsibilities at

_____

We the teachers do solemnly vow to...

Observation and Interview

Ask participants to observe an early childhood program that implements multicultural education and has been doing so for some time, noticing the staff roles and ways that multicultural education is integrated into the entire program. After observing, have participants interview one of the teachers. Participants can generate their own list of questions prior to the interview and report their findings to the class.

Five Year Plan

One way to deal with an enormous task is to break it down into manageable bits. Identifying long-range plans helps reduce staff anxiety and create a more realistic picture of what it takes to implement a multicultural curriculum. This activity is especially applicable for directors, who are responsible for strategic planning and need to be able to think in terms of long-term change. It can also work well as a group problem solving activity with a small to medium-sized staff.

1. List all the tasks that need to be accomplished in order to implement multicultural education at your site. Refer to "Steps to Implement Multicultural Education" on page 46 and the section "Integrating Multicultural Education into the Entire Program" on pages 46 - 48 in *Roots and Wings*.

2. Prioritize the tasks.

3. Identify how long each task will take to complete. Tasks can be measured by the number of hours, days, weeks, or months.

4. Analyze the list in terms of resources available. How much additional staff time is there? Are funds available? If so, how much? Are there other resources which can be tapped, like parents or volunteers?

5. Create a plan with six month goals, one year goals, two year goals, and five year goals.

6. Assign staff and resources to the plan.

7. Implement the plan. Evaluate and adjust the plan six months, one year, and two years from implementation.

Prioritized Task List for Implementing Multicultural Education

	Task	How long will it take?	Resources available
1.			
2.			
3.			
4.			
5.			
6.			
7.			
8.			
9.			
10.			
11.			
12.			
13.			
14.			
15.			
16.			
17.			
18.			
19.			
20.			

Six Month Goals

1.			
2.			
3.			
4.			
5.			

Prioritized Task List for Implementing Multicultural Education (cont.)

	Task	How long will it take?	Resources available
One Year Goals			
1.	_____	_____	_____
2.	_____	_____	_____
3.	_____	_____	_____
4.	_____	_____	_____
5.	_____	_____	_____
Two Year Goals			
1.	_____	_____	_____
2.	_____	_____	_____
3.	_____	_____	_____
4.	_____	_____	_____
5.	_____	_____	_____
Five Year Goals			
1.	_____	_____	_____
2.	_____	_____	_____
3.	_____	_____	_____
4.	_____	_____	_____
5.	_____	_____	_____
6.	_____	_____	_____
7.	_____	_____	_____
8.	_____	_____	_____
9.	_____	_____	_____
10.	_____	_____	_____

SESSION FIVE

Cultural Diversity through the Classroom

Description

Create a classroom that supports cultural diversity by learning how to recognize stereotypic materials, identifying ways to teach multicultural education through interest areas, rating your own environment, selecting materials to add to the classroom, and making a multicultural teaching aid.

Goals

1. Recognize the role of multicultural education.
2. Differentiate between stereotypic, nonstereotypic, and antistereotypic materials.
3. Examine ways to add multicultural materials to the classroom.
4. Evaluate a classroom for evidence of multicultural education.
5. Select action steps to take to increase the diversity present in the classroom.
6. Construct a multicultural visual aid.

Ice Breaker: What Do You Need to Feel at Home?   15 minutes

Begin the session with two stories. Ask participants to find a comfortable position. Tell them you are going to tell them two stories. They can listen with their eyes open or closed. Say:

Imagine you are a child and your parents have decided that it would be good for you to travel through space to visit another planet inhabited by civilized alien beings. You have been told about these aliens, but you still aren't quite sure what to expect. Upon landing on this foreign planet, you are greeted by the aliens. You are shocked and a little scared. These creatures look very different from you. They talk differently and interact with one another in very different ways.

They take you to one of their schools so that you can learn about their culture. You are excited about the opportunity. You like school and get along well with other kids. You eagerly walk up to the school entrance. The doors open automatically. That really surprises you, but you take a big breath and walk inside. The doors close behind you.

Immediately you get the feeling that you are not simply a visitor, but an alien being to these space creatures. They stare at you, point at you. Nothing in the school looks familiar to you. There isn't anyone there that speaks your language. The layout, the equipment, materials, activities, behaviors, and language make no sense to you. You are totally overwhelmed. You wish for something that you can relate to, something that looks or sounds familiar. By the end of the day, you have a headache and feel sick to your stomach. You just want to go home. Finally, a space creature arrives that speaks your language. It approaches you and asks if you are all right. You tell it that you just want to go home.

Ask participants to turn to the person sitting next to them and answer these questions: How did you feel being a child on another planet with alien space creatures? How did the school environment reinforce those feelings? What did you need to feel "at home" in the alien space creature's school?

After five minutes or so, tell the second story:

Imagine you are a young Hispanic child. Grandma has always taken care of you while your parents work. Now mom is going back to school and grandma can't take care of you anymore. Your mom has enrolled you in the campus child care center. You like the idea of going to big people's school with mom, but you also wish that you could stay with grandma.

On the first day of school, mom takes your hand and walks you into the child care center. She helps you find your cubbie. It has your name on it in Spanish and English. A woman walks up to the two of you, kneels down and says "Hi, I'm Joy, your new teacher. Welcome to our child care center." Mom smiles at you, gives you a big hug and kiss, and says "Good-bye Miguelito. I'll pick you up after nap." Joy takes your hand and shows you around the center. She tells you it's playtime and that you can play with anything you want.

First you notice the dramatic play area. You find a tortilla press, a griddle, and an empty masa container. Just like grandma's, you think to yourself. There are lots of baby dolls, and some of them look like you. They have shiny brown hair, big brown eyes, and light brown skin. Next you look at some picture books. Some of the books are new to you and some of them you've seen before. You especially like Rosie and Roo *and* Day Care A B C's. *You look up to see a poster of a man holding a little boy. The man reminds you of your grandpa and how he is big and strong and sometimes holds you.*

Kids are giggling at a table. You walk over to see what's so funny. The table is really a big plastic tub full of beans. You and grandma bought those kind of beans before, and she made burritos for you. The beans feel cool and bumpy. You bury your hands in the tub of beans. Just then Joy puts her arms around you, making you feel safe and warm inside. You can't wait to tell grandma about your new day care.

Again ask participants to turn to the person next to them and answer the questions: How did it feel being a Hispanic child in this center? How did the classroom environment reinforce those feelings? What did the center do to make you feel at home? In addition, ask them to share with each another what they've done to implement multicultural education in their classrooms.

Problem Posing: Role of the Environment   40 minutes

Large Group Discussion

Bring the class together. Ask participants to share highlights of their discussion. Weave together the themes that point to the importance of room arrangement and classroom materials to multicultural education. Consider asking questions like: What message do you hope your classroom gives to children and parents? How does the classroom environment relate to multicultural education?

Suggest that selection of good multicultural materials is critical to creating an environment that celebrates diversity. Present the group with three questions: How do you know what is stereotypic? How do you know what is nonstereotypic? How do you know what is antistereotypic? Write the questions across the chalkboard. Discuss each question one at a time, writing participants' answers in column form underneath the question. Encourage participants to identify a list of characteristics that would help them select and evaluate materials.

You may want to discuss stereotypic, nonstereotypic, and antistereotypic materials in terms of purpose and outcome. Pose questions like: Why does someone make this type of material? What does the designer hope will happen as a result of using the material? What probably happens to children as a result of using this type of material?

Codification: Identifying Stereotypic Materials

Divide the class into small groups of three to four participants. Give each group 2 - 4 multicultural teaching materials. These materials could be children's books, puzzles, posters, games, dramatic play props, art materials, a craft activity, or dolls. Ask the groups to examine their objects one at a time and answer these questions: What is it? What does it teach children? How would you use it? Is it stereotypic, nonstereotypic, or antistereotypic? If there is time, bring the groups together, asking each one to share their assessment of the multicultural teaching materials with the rest of the class.

Presentation of Content: Teaching through the
Classroom Environment   40 minutes

Mini-Lecture: Steps for Adding Multicultural Materials

Present a lecture on the five steps to follow when adding multicultural teaching materials and visual displays. Refer to page 56 in *Roots and Wings*. Make visual props to go with the lecture such as an overhead transparency listing interest areas, a poster showing the floor plan of a classroom divided into interest areas, a toys in an original container that is biased, samples of alternative storage containers, and samples of labels for shelves and interest areas.

Reading: Multicultural Education through Interest Centers

Ask participants to read the section on interest centers (pages 56 - 66 of *Roots and Wings*) in class and select three items they could add to each interest center in their classroom to increase the cultural diversity.

Critical Reflection: Rating Your Classroom   10 minutes

Give participants a chance to further reflect on the extent to which diversity is present in their classrooms. Distribute a copy of the handout "Multicultural Rating Scale." Ask participants to use the evaluation tool to rate their classroom and the results with one other person.

Multicultural Classroom Rating Scale

Directions: Use this rating scale to determine if you are implementing multicultural education through the classroom. Rate each interest area on a scale of 1 to 6 with 1 being the lowest rating and 6 being the highest. Read the descriptions for the 0, 2, 4, and 6 ratings. Circle the number above the description that best matches your classroom. Give yourself a rating of 1, 3, or 5 if your classroom falls between two descriptions. Tally your score on the last page of the rating scale.

	0	2	4	6
Art Area	no art area or art materials only in primary colors	art area with magazines, skin-color crayons, collage materials	add skin color paint, construction paper, red clay, fabric scraps	add skin color play dough, colors and patterns from other cultures, hand mirrors
Block Area	no block area, no block accessories or all Euro-American	block area with two or more types of blocks, multicultural people figures	add a variety of transportation toys and animals	add raw materials like cardboard boxes, canvas, string, tape, leaves, husks, sticks, stones
Music Area	no music area, or materials stored out of children's reach, poor selection of music	music area with a record player or tape recorders children can operate, a small selection of folk music, teach songs from other cultures, a set of rhythm instruments	add a wide variety of music, teach songs about diversity, acceptance, and cooperation, a variety of rhythm instruments	add music from children's homes, teach songs about taking action and fairness, a real drum
Dramatic Play	no dramatic play area, no multi-ethnic dolls, no full-length mirror	dramatic play area, a set of multi-ethnic dolls, full-length mirror, multi-ethnic hats	add multi-ethnic food containers, cooking utensils, eating utensils, clothing, shoes	add crates, large pieces of fabric, variety of floor plans, bedding, and misc. props
Table Toys	no table toy area, manipulatives stored out of children's reach, toys kept in original container	table toy area with multi-ethnic puzzles, toys out of original container	add games and activities that teach visual discrimination, alike and different, matching, sorting, and recognizing symbols	add games that teach whole-part relationships, one-to-one correspondence, sequencing.

Multicultural Classroom Rating Scale (cont.)

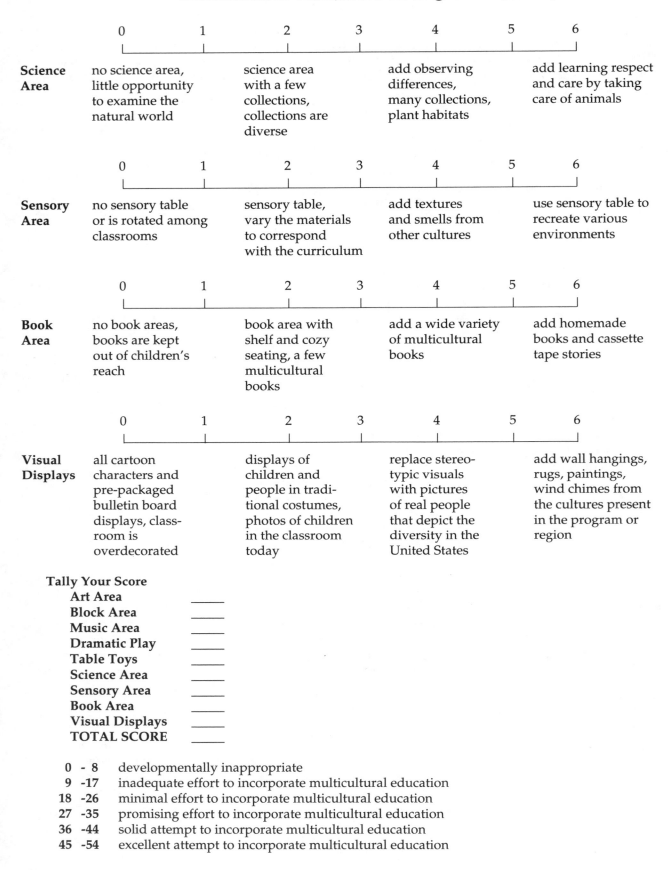

	0	1	2	3	4	5	6

Science Area — no science area, little opportunity to examine the natural world · science area with a few collections, collections are diverse · add observing differences, many collections, plant habitats · add learning respect and care by taking care of animals

	0	1	2	3	4	5	6

Sensory Area — no sensory table or is rotated among classrooms · sensory table, vary the materials to correspond with the curriculum · add textures and smells from other cultures · use sensory table to recreate various environments

	0	1	2	3	4	5	6

Book Area — no book areas, books are kept out of children's reach · book area with shelf and cozy seating, a few multicultural books · add a wide variety of multicultural books · add homemade books and cassette tape stories

	0	1	2	3	4	5	6

Visual Displays — all cartoon characters and pre-packaged bulletin board displays, classroom is overdecorated · displays of children and people in traditional costumes, photos of children in the classroom today · replace stereotypic visuals with pictures of real people that depict the diversity in the United States · add wall hangings, rugs, paintings, wind chimes from the cultures present in the program or region

Tally Your Score

Art Area	_____
Block Area	_____
Music Area	_____
Dramatic Play	_____
Table Toys	_____
Science Area	_____
Sensory Area	_____
Book Area	_____
Visual Displays	_____
TOTAL SCORE	_____

0 - 8	developmentally inappropriate
9 -17	inadequate effort to incorporate multicultural education
18 -26	minimal effort to incorporate multicultural education
27 -35	promising effort to incorporate multicultural education
36 -44	solid attempt to incorporate multicultural education
45 -54	excellent attempt to incorporate multicultural education

Practical Application: Making a Multicultural Visual Display   **60 minutes**

Set out poster board, scissors, glue, felt tip markers and a variety of magazines. Consider asking participants to bring their own magazines if you don't have access to a wide variety. You might also provide clear contact paper so they can make their visual display durable. Give participants 45 minutes to an hour to make a multicultural visual display for their classroom.

Journaling

1. How are your program's goals reflected in the classroom?
2. How are your own attitudes and values reflected in your classroom?

Affirmations

Symbol: crayon

1. I teach through the classroom environment.
2. My classroom conveys acceptance.
3. I celebrate diversity in my classroom.
4. I remove stereotypic materials from my classroom.
5. I fill my classroom with nonstereotypic and antistereotypic materials.
6. I choose visual displays that depict real life.
7. I use my imagination and creativity to design teaching materials.
8. I enjoy locating multicultural resources.
9. I enjoy making multicultural teaching materials.

Additional Activities

Exhibit of Multicultural Materials

Set out an extensive display of multicultural materials that are appropriate for early childhood classrooms. Give participants an opportunity to examine the materials.

Guest Speaker

Invite a children's bookseller, educational materials supplier, or a children's librarian to present their collection of multicultural materials to the class.

Field Trip

Arrange a class field trip to a local children's bookstore, educational supply center, poster shop, or multicultural resource center. Try to find one that is quite willing to have your students visit their shop, show their posters, and give some background on the posters that represent historical events and social/political movement.

Evaluate Children's Books

Use the form, "What Are We Really Saying to Children?" on pages 57-58 in *Roots and Wings* to evaluate children's books. You may want to have participants work in pairs or small groups. Ask them to present their finding to the rest of the class.

Relating the Classroom to Children's Lives

Ask participants to consider how their classroom relates to the real lives of the children by asking themselves: How is your classroom like the child's home environment? How is your classroom different from the child's home environment? How is your classroom like the child's neighborhood? How is it different from the child's neighborhood?

Selecting Materials to Support the Goals

This activity will help teachers identify materials that support the goals of multicultural education. Distribute the handout "Support Your Goals through Multicultural Materials." Ask participants to review educational supply catalogs and complete the assignment.

Support Your Goals through Multicultural Materials

Directions: You have received a grant of $500.00 to improve the multicultural resources in your classroom. Use this form to help you select $500.00 worth of materials to support the goals of multicultural education.

Multicultural Goals	Materials to Support Goals	Cost
1. Recognize the beauty, value, and contribution of each child.		
2. Foster high self-esteem and a positive self-concept.		
3. Teach children about their own culture.		
4. Introduce children to other cultures.		
5. Provide a positive experience exploring similarities and differences.		
6. Encourage children to respect other cultures.		
7. Increase children's ability to talk to and play with people who are different from them.		
8. Help children to be a group member.		
9. Talk about racism.		
10. Talk about current events.		
11. Help children live in a diverse world.		
12. Help children notice and do something about unfair behavior.		
	Total Cost:	

Locating and Rating Multicultural Materials

Early childhood teachers often ask me, "Where did you find that?" I'm a collector and resourcer by nature, so locating multicultural materials comes easy to me. This activity will help teachers determine the availability and quality of multicultural materials available. Use it to focus on local resources. Send participants out into the community to assess the availability and quality of multicultural materials. Consider following it with a review of mail order resources, especially if the participant's research turns up a real lack of appropriate materials in your community.

Have the class refer back to the criteria of stereotypic, nonstereotypic, and anti-stereotypic materials they generated during the problem-posing portion of the class session. Use their criteria to create a checklist that participants can use to evaluate materials. Type up the checklist and distribute five copies to each participant.

Assign participants to visit a local store and select five multicultural materials that would be appropriate for young children. Consider passing around a list of stores and asking participants to select which one to visit. This way, the entire group will learn about what is available in a variety of places. While in the store, participants should examine the materials and complete the checklist. Ask them to bring the completed checklists to class. Give each person an opportunity to present his or her findings. Then facilitate a large group discussion on the availability, appropriateness, quality, and cost of multicultural materials. Participants may find that some of the best items are found in the most unusual places.

Evaluating Catalog Resources

Currently, mail order catalogs are the best source of multicultural materials, and teachers need an opportunity to become familiar with these catalogs and the materials available. Send for catalogs from the suppliers listed on pages 67 - 71 in *Roots and Wings*. Gather any other early childhood supply catalogs. Set the catalogs out on a table and ask each participant to take one. Distribute copies of the checklist created in the previous activity. Ask each person to choose five catalog items to rate using the checklist.

Planning Multicultural Curriculum

Description

Identify curriculum themes that lend themselves to multicultural education, and learn how to expand themes to include multicultural goals and concepts.

Goals

1. Identify characteristics of developmentally appropriate curriculum themes.
2. Associate curriculum themes with multicultural education.
3. Select a theme to develop into a curriculum unit.
4. Identify and list the concepts presented to children in this curriculum theme.
5. Evaluate the thematic concepts according to the goals of multicultural education.
6. Develop a unit theme using the curriculum planning form.

Ice Breaker: How Do You Plan Curriculum?   15 minutes

Ask participants to form a small group of three to four and discuss the following questions:

1. *How do you plan your curriculum?*
2. *How might you plan multicultural curriculum?*
3. *In terms of multicultural curriculum, what messages do you want to convey to young children?*

Bring the group together and ask participants to share their answer to the question "How might you organize multicultural curriculum?" Emphasize that multicultural curriculum planning does not require a new, unique, or different approach. You may want to briefly describe environmentally based curriculum planning if this is a new concept to participants.

Problem Posing: What are Multicultural Themes?   15 minutes

Ask participants to brainstorm themes that provide children with an opportunity to explore multicultural concepts. List the themes on the board or on chart paper. (This list should be displayed throughout the class session.) Next, ask participants to brainstorm a list of themes that do not provide an opportunity to explore multicultural concepts. Write this list beside the list of themes that reinforce multicultural concepts. Ask participants to review the list. Pose the question "What makes a theme supportive of or contradictory to multicultural education?" If participants need help with this question, encourage them to notice the similarities or shared characteristics of the themes on each list. Encourage participants to use this information to help them select unit themes for their classroom.

Presentation of Content: Incorporating Multicultural Concepts into Unit Themes   20 minutes

Use cognitive webbing to help participants identify the concepts and content of unit themes. Cognitive webbing is a nonlinear approach to generating and organizing ideas. Ask the class to select one theme to develop into a curriculum unit. Write the title of the theme in the center of the chalkboard. Ask: What can children learn about (*name of theme*)? What do children want to know about (*name of theme*)? How do young children experience (*name of theme*)? What issues are children working on related to (*name of theme*)? What about (*name of theme*) confuses children?

Write participants' ideas around the theme title. Group related ideas together to form subthemes. You can create the image of a web by drawing lines to connect the ideas. See the example of a web that one of my classes created for the unit theme "Friends." If this is an ongoing class, you can copy the webbing from the chalkboard, create a handout, and distribute it to participants at the next class session. Sometimes I take the information and put it in outline form. See the example of a curriculum theme based on pets on page 74 of *Roots and Wings*.

Friends Unit in Cognitive Webbing Form

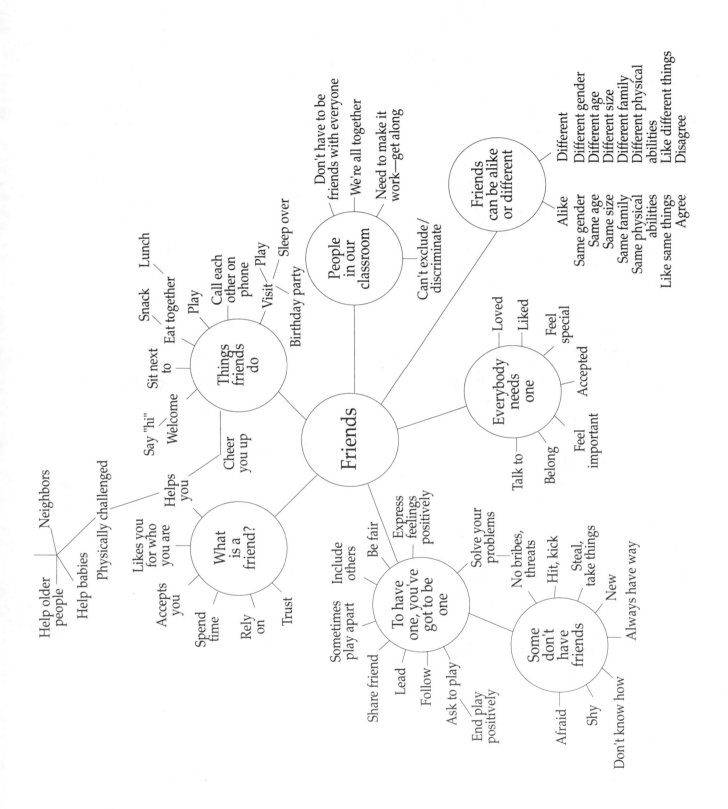

Friends Unit in Outline Form

A. What is a friend?
1. A friend is somebody you can trust.
2. A friend is somebody you can rely on.
3. A friend is somebody who listens to you.
4. A friend is somebody you spend time with.
5. A friend is somebody who accepts you as you are, not for what you have or what you wear.
6. A friend is somebody who helps you.

B. Friends can be alike.
1. Boys are friends with boys. Girls are friends with girls.
2. Friends are the same age.
3. Friends are the same size.
4. Friends look alike. Example: same skin color, facial features.
5. Friends can be in the same family. Example: cousins.
6. Friends talk alike.
7. Friends have the same physical abilities.
8. Friends like the same things.
9. Friends agree with one another.

C. Friends can be different.
1. Boys are friends with girls. Girls are friends with boys.
2. Friends are different ages.
3. Friends are different sizes.
4. Friends come from different families.
5. Friends have different physical abilities.
6. Friends like different things.
7. Friends disagree with one another.

D. Everybody needs a friend.
1. We all need to belong.
2. We all need to feel accepted.
3. We all need to be liked and loved.
4. We all need someone we can talk to.
5. We all need to feel important and special.

E. To have a friend, you have to be one.
1. Use positive ways to ask a friend to play.
2. Sometimes be a follower.
3. Sometimes be a leader.
4. Share your friend. Let your friend play with others.
5. Sometimes play together and sometimes play apart.
6. Invite others to play with you and your friend.
7. Play fair.
8. Express your feelings positively.
9. Solve your problems.
10. Don't bribe or threaten your friend.
11. End your play positively.

F. **Some people don't have friends.**
   1. They use their body to hurt others.
   2. They take things from others.
   3. They play unfairly.
   4. They must always have their way.
   5. They are shy or afraid of others.
   6. They don't know how to play with others.
   7. They are new and haven't made any friends yet.

G. **Things friends do.**
   1. Greet each other.
   2. Sit next to each other.
   3. Play together.
   4. Share toys.
   5. Eat with each other.
   6. Call each other on the phone.
   7. Visit each other's homes.
   8. Sleep over at each other's houses.
   9. Cheer each other up.

H. **Friends help others.**
   1. We can be friends to babies and younger children.
   2. We can be friends to older adults.
   3. We can be friends to people from other cultures.
   4. We can be friends to physically challenged children.
   5. We can be friends to homeless people.
   6. We can be friends to animals.
   7. We can be friends to our neighbors.
   8. We can be friends to our community.
   9. We can be friends to children in other countries.
   10. We can be friends to the earth.

I. **Classroom friends.**
   1. You don't have to be friends with everyone.
   2. Because we are all together, we have to get along.
   3. You may not exclude someone because of their skin color.
   4. You may not exclude someone because of their facial features.
   5. You may not exclude someone because of how they talk.
   6. You may not exclude someone because of age.
   7. You may not exclude someone because of their physical ability.

Critical Reflection: Does This Theme Incorporate Multicultural Goals? 15 minutes

Distribute a copy of the handout "Evaluating Curriculum Themes." Ask participants to review their curriculum web and decide if the theme, as developed by the class, incorporates the goals of multicultural education. Tell them to use the form to help them make their decision. If there are any goals that are not met, participants should make revisions so that the theme meets the goals of multicultural education. Present this exercise as an individual or small group activity.

Evaluating Multicultural Themes

Curriculum Theme_____

	Multicultural Goal	Yes	No	Comment
1.	Does it recognize the beauty, value, and contribution of each child?	_____	_____	_____ _____
2.	Does it foster high self-esteem and a positive self-concept?	_____	_____	_____ _____
3.	Does it acknowledge similarities?	_____	_____	_____ _____
4.	Does it acknowledge diversity?	_____	_____	_____ _____
5.	Does it teach children about their own culture?	_____	_____	_____ _____
6.	Does it promote awareness of other cultures?	_____	_____	_____ _____
7.	Does it promote respect towards other cultures?	_____	_____	_____ _____
8.	Does it increase children's ability to interact with people who are different from them?	_____	_____	_____ _____
9.	Does it help children to be a group member?	_____	_____	_____ _____
10.	Does it teach children how to cooperate with others?	_____	_____	_____ _____
11.	Does it promote group problem solving?	_____	_____	_____ _____
12.	Does it help children notice prejudice?	_____	_____	_____ _____
13.	Does it teach children how to challenge prejudice?	_____	_____	_____ _____

Practical Application: Planning Multicultural Curriculum
90 minutes

Mini-Lecture: Using the "Curriculum Planning Form"

Distribute a copy of the "Curriculum Planning Form" to each participant. Explain the purpose of each section and how to use the form. Refer to pages 74 - 77 in *Roots and Wings* to help you prepare the mini-lecture.

Small Group Curriculum Planning

Divide the class into small groups of four to five participants. Ask each group to plan a unit based on the theme and concepts previously identified by the class. Set aside an hour of class time for participants to plan their unit. Refer participants to sections of *Roots and Wings* that will assist them in planning the unit. The calendar in Chapter Six will help participants identify special dates. Pages 145 - 146 list ideas for field trips and visitors. A comprehensive list of materials to add to interest centers is located on pages 59 - 63.

Introduce participants to and set out additional curriculum resource books such as *Anti-Bias Curriculum, Open the Door, Let's Explore, Activities Handbook for Teachers of Young Children, Art for the Fun of It, The Cooperative Sports and Games Book, Don't Move the Muffin Tins, Scribble Cookies, The Outside Play and Learning Book, Mudpies to Magnets*, and *I Can Do It! I Can Do It!* You may also want to set out educational materials catalogs, children's book catalogs, or a bibliography of multicultural children's books.

Ask each group to share their unit plan with the class. Make copies of each of the unit plans and distribute them to class participants.

Curriculum Planning Form

Theme: _____

Weeks/Month: _____

Basic Concepts: _____

_____

Special Dates: _____

Field Trips/Visitors: _____

Cooking Activities/Snack: _____

Visual Displays: _____

Parent Newsletter: _____

Classroom Environment

Book Area: _____

Art Area: _____

Block Area: _____

Small Muscle/Manipulative Area: _____

Dramatic Play Area: _____

Music/Movement Area: _____

Sand/Water Table: _____

Science Table: _____

Playground/Gym: _____

Journaling

1. Of the curriculum themes identified in *Roots and Wings* and your class, which ones are already part of your curriculum?
2. What are your thoughts about the curriculum developed and the process used in this class?
3. Review the curriculum developed in this class. How might your life be different if you had been taught these concepts as a child?

Affirmations

Symbol: apple

1. I plan multicultural curriculum.
2. I choose curriculum themes that support multicultural values.
3. I incorporate multicultural goals and concepts into my unit themes.
4. I avoid "tourist" themes.
5. I eliminate "tourist" themes from my curriculum.
6. I actively participate in curriculum planning as a member of my teaching team.
7. I individualize the curriculum.

Additional Activities

Individualized Planning

Use the "Individualized Planning Form" to help participants individualize their curriculum. Distribute the four copies of the form, 10-20 slips of paper, and a paper bag to each participant. Ask them to write the name of each child in their class on a slip of paper and place the names inside the paper bag. Next ask them to randomly select the four names and complete the planning form for each child. You might want to consider requiring participants to observe each child prior to completing the "Individualized Planning Form."

Ask participants to share the results of this exercise with one other person in the class and discuss these questions: What did you learn from this exercise? How will you incorporate this information into the curriculum?

Individualized Planning Form

1. Write the name of each child in your class on a piece of paper. Fold each slip of paper and place it in a paper bag. Mix up the slips and then draw four slips.

2. Write the names of the children selected on the forms, using one form for each child.

3. Reflect on each child's development and culture. You may need to refer to the child's enrollment file. Spend 30 minutes describing each child. Write your comments on the form.

Development

A. Large and small muscle

B. Language

C. Intellectual

D. Emotional

E. Social

Culture

A. Cultural background and customs

B. Child's home life

C. Child's favorite foods

D. Child's preferred way of expressing self and comforting self

E. Favorite objects, toys, things to talk about—in other words, what does this child enjoy?

F. Child's favorite areas in the center, favorite activity

If you were going to plan a day just for this child, what would it be like? What would you do when the child arrived? What would be the sequence and duration of the activities?

Adapted from Williams, Leslie R. and Yvonne DeGaetano, *Alerta: A Multicultural, Bilingual Approach to Teaching Young Children.* Menlo Park: Addison Wesley, 1985.

Interview

Interview a teacher who implements multicultural curriculum. Ask her how she currently organizes and plans curriculum. What other methods has she tried in the past? How did she come to select the method she is currently using? How does she identify and incorporate the needs and interests of individual children? How does she avoid falling into a tourist approach?

Plan a Curriculum Unit

Using the process and curriculum planning form presented in this session, ask participants to plan a curriculum unit that incorporates multicultural goals. Have them present their plan to the class. Copy and distribute each of the curriculum plans to the class participants, so that they all leave the course with a curriculum packet.

Evaluate a Curriculum Unit

Ask participants to select one curriculum unit from their own files, evaluate it for consistency with multicultural goals, and revise it to incorporate cultural diversity. Give participants the handout "Evaluating Multicultural Themes," and ask them to use it to evaluate their curriculum unit.

Implement a Multicultural Unit

Select one of the multicultural curriculum units developed to implement. Ask participants to implement the unit for one week to one month. Bring the participants together to report what they did and how the children responded. Through small group discussions, encourage participants to give feedback to one another and evaluate the results.

Learning from Mistakes

Everybody makes mistakes. It is very difficult to implement multicultural education without making some mistakes along the way. In addition, we can learn from each other's mistakes. Here's an opportunity to turn mistakes into learning experiences. Ask participants to identify three mistakes they made in trying to implement multicultural curriculum. Next, encourage them to reflect on what they learned from those mistakes. Ask: What would you do differently next time? How could you have prevented the situation?

How Would They Design Multicultural Curriculum?

This is an exercise in creative thinking adapted from Roger von Oech's *Creative Whack Pack*. Ask the participants to identify who they respect in early childhood education and who they look up to. Then imagine how those respected or famous early childhood folks would design and implement multicultural curriculum for young children. Here are some examples:

How might Maria Montessori teach children about culture?

How might David Weikert or the people at the High/Scope Foundation teach children about culture?

How might Dr. Barry Brazelton teach children about culture?

You could also consider how celebrities or recent heroes might implement multicultural education:

How would Mr. Rogers teach children about culture?

How would Sesame Street teach children about culture?

How would Bill Cosby teach children about culture?

How would Martin Luther King, Jr. teach children about culture?

How would Malcolm X teach children about culture?

SESSION SEVEN

Simple Activities You Can Use to Teach Multicultural Awareness

Description

A practical class, focusing on activities teachers can use in their classrooms. Learn how to adapt many common and developmentally appropriate activities to help young children identify, accept, and appreciate cultural diversity.

Goals

1. Identify developmentally appropriate activities.
2. Relate multicultural activities to child development.
3. Examine concepts and skills children can gain through multicultural education.
4. Evaluate and adapt an early childhood activity to support multicultural education.
5. Select and implement a multicultural activity from *Roots and Wings*.
6. Create a community resource file of multicultural field trips, visitors, and special events.

Ice Breaker: How Did You Learn about the World?   10 minutes

As participants arrive, ask them to find a partner and discuss how they learned about the world. What were they taught in elementary school? What were they taught in junior high school? What were they taught in high school? What kinds of activities do they remember their teachers using to teach about other cultures, countries, and geography? Ask participants to share some of their experiences with the group and acknowledge that when we think of multicultural education we may envision these types of activities. As a result, it can be hard to determine appropriate activities for young children.

Problem Posing: How Do We Know How to Choose Multicultural Activities for Young Children?   30 minutes

Brainstorming

Encourage the group to use child development as the basis for selecting, designing, and rejecting possible activities to teach multicultural concepts. Therefore, if their program is already using a child-centered, developmentally appropriate, or cognitively oriented curriculum, their activities are likely to reflect accepted child development principles.

Write the major areas of child development across the top of the chalkboard. I use these categories: social, emotional, language, cognitive, sensory, creative, motor. Mention that early childhood education seeks to teach to the whole child and uses educational activities to promote development in each of these areas.

Ask participants to brainstorm common activities that they use to promote development in each of these areas. For example, under cognitive development you might identify labeling, sorting, matching, classifying, sequencing, and counting as possible activities. Then ask: "How can you use these activities to teach multicultural concepts or develop cultural awareness?"

Small Group Discussion

Distribute a copy of the handout "Classifying Multicultural Activities." Divide the class into small groups of three to four and ask them to sort the activities listed at the top of the handout into three categories: activities to avoid, activities to limit, and activities to implement. Encourage them to refer back to the list of activities generated through the brainstorming session and their discussion of how they were taught about cultures in making their decisions regarding the appropriateness of activities.

Classifying Multicultural Activities

Directions

Sort the following activities into three categories: activities you would avoid presenting to young children, activities you would limit, and activities you would present to young children. Answer the questions at the bottom of the page.

Possible Activities

skin color play dough
make face masks
look at cultural artifacts
learn about revolutions
explore light and dark
look at family photos
compare real and pretend
matching patterns
learn about presidents
draw each other
make puppets of children
in costume

skin color finger painting
learn names of countries
compare and chart physical
features
make a felt doll of each child
identify similarities among
people
make costumes
identify people by their voice
celebrate a foreign holiday
make books about ourselves

skin color collages
taste foreign foods
find countries on maps
color ditto sheet of a flag
read a folk tale
learn a folk dance
identify own skin color
pretend to be "Japanese"
invite parents to share their culture
learn about hair
taste different breads

Activities to Avoid	Activities to Limit	Activities to Include

1. Which activities were easy to sort? Which ones were more difficult?

2. What makes it hard to decide if an activity is appropriate for young children?

3. What activities did your group agree on? Which activities did you disagree on?

Presentation of Content: Identifying Appropriate Multicultural Concepts and Skills for Young Children   20 minutes

Present a brief lecture on the multicultural concepts that children can understand. The list of concepts appears on pages 79 and 82 in *Roots and Wings*. Consider making an overhead transparency or handout listing these concepts. Next identify and explain the cognitive and social skills children can develop through a developmentally appropriate approach to multicultural education. The list of skills is on page 82 in *Roots and Wings*. Try to provide concrete examples of activities that foster these skills. You might want to make some sample activities for participants to examine.

Critical Reflection: Self-Examination and Evaluating an Activity   30 minutes

Guided Imagery: The Wise Owl

Ask participants to find a comfortable sitting position. Encourage them to relax their body by rotating their shoulders and head, and letting their arms hang loosely with their hands resting in their lap. Tell them to breathe deeply and slowly, releasing any tension as they exhale. Then say:

Close your eyes and see yourself preparing activities for a group of young children. Imagine a friendly owl resting comfortably on your shoulder. The owl is known for its wisdom and ability to see things that others cannot see. Owls have great insight and always speak the truth. Ask your owl friend to help you with planning and implementing multicultural activities. Listen to what the owl has to say to you.

*

How can you be more like the owl? What truth or truths do you need to speak as a teacher of young children?

*

What signals are the children giving you that you need to be aware of? How can you incorporate this awareness into your curriculum?

*

What are you afraid of? Are you afraid of making a mistake or hurting someone's feelings? This type of thinking is a trap. Ask the wise owl to help you break free so that you can tell the truth and help children grow.

*

Now it's time to say good-bye to the owl. Thank the owl for helping you today. Remember the owl and imagine it perched on your shoulder when you need insight or the courage to speak the truth. When you are ready, open your eyes and join me in this room.

Evaluating Multicultural Activities

Ask participants to write up a multicultural activity they have used prior to this workshop or course. Distribute a blank activity form and a copy of the handout "Evaluating Multicultural Activities" to each participant. Ask them to write up their activity on the activity form. Once they have written up the activity, ask them to exchange activities with someone else in the class and use the handout to evaluate the multicultural activity. Once they have completed the evaluation, ask them to return the activity along with the evaluation form to their fellow class members.

Activity Planning Form

Title: _____

_____

Themes: _____

_____

Goal: _____

_____

Materials: _____

_____

_____

_____

_____

Description: _____

_____

_____

_____

_____

_____

_____

_____

Variation: _____

_____

_____

_____

_____

_____

_____

Evaluating Multicultural Activities

Activity_____

	Item	Yes	No	Comment
1.	Is the content developmentally appropriate?	_____	_____	_____
2.	Are the methods developmentally appropriate?	_____	_____	_____
3.	Does it contain stereotypes?	_____	_____	_____
4.	Does it recognize the beauty, value, and contribution of each child?	_____	_____	_____
5.	Does it foster high self-esteem and a positive self-concept?	_____	_____	_____
6.	Does it acknowledge similarities?	_____	_____	_____
7.	Does it acknowledge diversity?	_____	_____	_____
8.	Does it teach children about their own culture?	_____	_____	_____
9.	Does it promote awareness of other cultures?	_____	_____	_____
10.	Does it promote respect towards other cultures?	_____	_____	_____
11.	Does it increase children's ability to interact with people who are different from them?	_____	_____	_____
12.	Does it help children to be a group member?	_____	_____	_____
13.	Does it teach children how to cooperate with others?	_____	_____	_____
14.	Does it promote group problem solving?	_____	_____	_____
15.	Does it help children notice prejudice?	_____	_____	_____
16.	Does it teach children how to challenge prejudice?	_____	_____	_____

Practical Application: Implementing
Multicultural Activities   60 minutes

Select four to six activities presented on pages 84 - 144 in *Roots and Wings*. You may want to choose one activity from each of the major areas: Exploring the Concept of Skin Color, Noticing Physical Characteristics, Exploring Racial and Ethnic Constancy, Exploring Similarities and Differences, Developing Social Skills, and Experiencing Culture in the Context of Daily Life. Gather and prepare the materials needed to implement the activities.

Divide the class into small groups of five people and assign each group an activity to implement. Tell the groups to review the activity in *Roots and Wings*, select one member to play the role of teacher, and the rest of the group will play the role of young children. Give them 10-15 minutes to run through the activity and make any final preparations of the materials.

Give each group an opportunity to present their activity to the rest of the class, who observe the "teacher" implementing a multicultural activity with her "children." Give the class an opportunity to discuss each activity after it has been presented. The following questions might help generate group discussion: For what age group would this activity work? What did you like about the activity? What might you change or do differently? Do you think this activity would work in your program? Could you see yourself implementing this activity? Ask the "teacher": How did it feel to present this activity to a group of "children?" Ask the participants pretending to be the children: "How did it feel to take part in this activity? Do you think children would enjoy it? Would they get anything out of it?"

Journaling

1. What did the owl say to you in the guided imagery?
2. Recall a time when the children in your class were confused by current events happening in another part of the world. What was the event? What was confusing to the children?
3. Recall a time when the children in your class were confused by historical events. What were you or another teacher trying to teach the children? What confused them or went over their heads?

Affirmations

Symbol: owl

1. I help children understand that people of other cultures live in our community today.
2. I limit the number of activities that focus on the unique and eccentric characteristics of a culture.
3. I provide opportunities for children to be active learners.
4. I provide opportunities for children to learn through all their senses.
5. I help children understand multicultural concepts.
6. I avoid making broad overgeneralizations when introducing multicultural materials and activities.

7. I provide many real experiences for children.
8. I trust that children will learn facts and important information about geography and other countries and cultures in elementary school, junior high school, and high school.

Additional Activities

Assessing Multicultural Skills

Use the following checklist to determine the presence of specific skills related to multicultural education. Ask participants to observe and record a child's behavior using the checklist "Child Skills for Living in a Multicultural Society." Then in a subsequent class session, have participants form small groups, share their results, interpret the data collected, and plan a response by identifying multicultural activities appropriate for the child.

Child Skills for Living in a Multicultural Society

Child_____Age_____Birthdate_____

Ethnicity_____Social Class_____Gender_____

Observer_____

Skill	Example	Date Observed
Sense of Self		
recognizes own beauty	_____	_____
recognizes own gifts and talents	_____	_____
recognizes everyone is important	_____	_____
shows pride	_____	_____
protects self	_____	_____
Emotional Skills		
notices and labels feelings	_____	_____
expresses feelings appropriately	_____	_____
demonstrates sensitivity to others	_____	_____
copes with change	_____	_____
tries new experiences	_____	_____
Social Skills		
trusts adults	_____	_____
respects others/other cultures	_____	_____
takes turns	_____	_____
shares with others	_____	_____
is a friend	_____	_____
participates in group activities	_____	_____
cooperates with others	_____	_____

Child Skills for Living in a Multicultural Society (cont.)

Skill	Example	Date Observed
Social Skills (cont.)		
practices leading and following	_____	_____
resolves conflicts	_____	_____
knows about own culture	_____	_____
aware of other cultures	_____	_____
Moral Reasoning and Social Action Skills		
helps others	_____	_____
asks for help	_____	_____
respects authority	_____	_____
follows rules	_____	_____
participates in making rules	_____	_____
avoids name-calling	_____	_____
notices fair and unfair behavior	_____	_____
takes action against unfair situations	_____	_____
participates in group activism	_____	_____
Problem-Solving Skills		
explores with all senses	_____	_____
observes objects from different points of view	_____	_____
examines alternatives	_____	_____
makes choices	_____	_____
predicts outcomes	_____	_____
explores cause and effect	_____	_____
evaluates outcomes	_____	_____

Child Skills for Living in a Multicultural Society (cont.)

Skill	Example	Date Observed

Cognitive Skills

    observes attributes of objects   _____ _____

    describes characteristics   _____ _____

    matches objects/people   _____ _____

    compares objects/people   _____ _____

    classifies objects/people   _____ _____

    differentiates objects/people   _____ _____

    explains characteristics   _____ _____

Literacy and Language Skills

    listens to others   _____ _____

    recognizes people by voice   _____ _____

    notices differences in language   _____ _____

    uses words to express self   _____ _____

    answers questions with words   _____ _____

    talks with others   _____ _____

    recognizes, matches visual patterns   _____ _____

    recognizes printed materials   _____ _____

    listens to stories   _____ _____

    recognizes own name   _____ _____

    matches objects with symbols   _____ _____

    sees own words in writing   _____ _____

Implement a Multicultural Activity

Ask participants to select one children's activity from *Roots and Wings* to implement in their own classrooms. Tell them to prepare the necessary materials, implement the activity at an interest center during free play or during a small group time. Remind them that these activities are not designed for large groups of 15 - 20 children to do together at the same time. You might want to ask participants to write up a brief evaluation of the activity and identify any variations they would make in the activity. Give participants an opportunity to share the results with the rest of the class.

Design Your Own Multicultural Activity

Consider asking participants to design and implement their own multicultural activity. Distribute a copy of the "Multicultural Activity Planning Form" to each person. Use this exercise only if participants have a solid understanding of multicultural education and previous experience implementing multicultural activities. Otherwise, it can be a set-up for failure. I have given this assignment before a group was ready, and 30 percent of the participants designed and implemented "tourist" activities! Set aside time in class for participants to present their activity and make copies of all the activities for the participants so that they leave the class with a new set of multicultural activities.

Write a Song or a Fingerplay

Currently there are very few appropriate songs or fingerplays for early childhood multicultural education. This activity gives teachers an opportunity to create new songs and fingerplays to use in their own classrooms. Divide the class into small groups of three to four. Ask each group to identify a topic related to multicultural education (use the goals on pages 24 - 25 and the concepts children can learn on pages 79 - 82 of *Roots and Wings*). Then ask them to create the lyrics to a song or the words and motions to a fingerplay that relate to the topic they have chosen. You might want to list the titles of familiar children's songs with simple tunes such as "Twinkle, Twinkle Little Star;" "Row, Row, Row Your Boat;" "Mary Had a Little Lamb;" "The Farmer in the Dell;" and "Jingle Bells." Participants can create a multicultural song by writing new lyrics to an old familiar tune. Also set out a thesaurus, rhyming dictionary, and musical instruments as additional resources. Give the small groups 30 minutes to create their song or fingerplay and set aside enough time so that they can lead the entire class in singing the song or reciting the fingerplay. Again, make copies of the songs and fingerplays so that each participant leaves the class with some new multicultural resources.

Create a Special Activities Resource File

Ask participants to read the special activities section on pages 145 - 146 of *Roots and Wings*. Have them create a resource file of special multicultural activities. Tell them to divide the resource file into three sections: walks, field trips, and visitors. They could add a fourth section of additional activities that would include activities such as pen pals and adopting another classroom. Establish a format for participants to use in developing their resource files. Some instructors prefer index cards and file boxes, others notebook paper in three-ring binders. Also identify for participants the type of information they need to gather and record for each resource. You might want to create a form that participants can follow in writing up their special activities and resources. Include information like activity title, name of contact person, address, phone number, cost, hours and days of operation, and description of services. Also ask participants to identify introductory activities, discussion questions, follow-up activities, and related curriculum resources.

Using a Planning Matrix

Lois Brokering, an early childhood consultant, advocates the use of a developmental matrix for curriculum planning. I have created a planning matrix for multicultural education that combines the content of chapters 4 and 5 in *Roots and Wings*. Introduce the matrix to participants who have examined both teaching through the classroom environment and activities for teaching children about culture. Lois suggests that teachers use a matrix as they plan their curriculum. As they identify materials to add to the interest areas, put a dot under the growth areas that will be fostered by the multicultural materials. Likewise, with each activity that is selected for a given theme, put a dot under the growth areas that are enhanced by the activity. This process allows teachers to identify the strengths and weaknesses of their curriculum plan and shows them where they need to make adjustments. The results may show, for example, that nothing is being offered in the sensory area, or many of the activities have a strong social skills emphasis but are weak in promoting cognitive skills.

Distribute a copy of the "Multicultural Curriculum Planning Matrix" to each of the participants. You might want to duplicate it on card stock and supply clear contact paper so that they can protect the matrix and make it reusable. (A crayon dot on clear contact paper can be wiped off with a tissue.)

Explain the matrix. Ask participants to evaluate a multicultural curriculum plan using the matrix. You could also divide the class into small groups and ask them to plan a unit using an appropriate theme, identifying materials for the interest areas, and multicultural activities. Then ask them to evaluate their own unit using the curriculum planning matrix.

Adapted from Brokering, Lois Redelfs, *Room To Grow*. Minneapolis: Augsburg Publishing House, 1988.

Multicultural Curriculum Planning Matrix

Category	Objective	LARGE GROUP	SMALL GROUP	PLAYGROUND/GYM	SCIENCE	SAND/WATER	MUSIC/MOVEMENT	DRAMATIC PLAY	MANIPULATIVE	BLOCK AREA	ART AREA	BOOK AREA	COOKING	FIELD TRIP, VISITOR	HOLIDAYS, CELEBRA.
SELF CONCEPT	RECOGNIZE OWN BEAUTY														
	RECOGNIZE OWN GIFTS/TALENTS														
	RECOGNIZE EVERYONE IMPORTANT														
	SHOW PRIDE IN SELF														
EMOTIONAL	LABEL AND EXPRESS FEELINGS														
	DEMONSTRATE SENSITIVITY														
	COPE WITH CHANGE														
	TRY NEW EXPERIENCE														
SOCIAL	RESPECT OTHERS														
	LEARN ABOUT DAILY LIFE														
	LEARN ABOUT OWN CULTURE														
	LEARN ABOUT OTHER CULTURES														
	TAKES TURNS/SHARES														
	COOPERATES WITH OTHERS														
	LEADS, FOLLOWS														
MORAL	HELPS OTHERS, ASK FOR HELP														
	NOTICE FAIR AND UNFAIR														
	TAKE GROUP ACTION														
PROBLEM SOLVING	EXPLORE WITH ALL SENSES														
	TAKE DIFFERENT VIEWPOINTS														
	EXAMINE ALTERNATIVES														
	MAKE CHOICES														
	EXPLORE CAUSE AND EFFECT														
COGNITIVE	OBSERVE, DESCRIBE ATTRIBUTES														
	MATCHING														
	COMPARE/ALIKE & DIFFERENT														
	CLASSIFY														
	EXPLAIN CHARACTERISTICS														
LANGUAGE	LISTENING														
	RECOGNIZING VOICES														
	TALKING, EXPRESS SELF														
	RECOGNIZE NAME														
	MATCH OBJECTS WITH SYMBOL														
	SEE OWN WORDS WRITTEN														

SESSION EIGHT

Multicultural Holidays and Celebrations

Description

Explore the benefits and risks of celebrating holidays in the classroom. Examine issues related to holidays and celebrations. Identify many holidays and learn how to incorporate holidays and celebrations into multicultural curriculum.

Goals

1. Identify your own feelings about holidays and celebrations.
2. Define holiday, celebration, and ritual.
3. Identify the purpose of holidays and celebrations.
4. Examine the role of holidays and celebrations in multicultural education.
5. Relate holiday activities to the different approaches to multicultural education.
6. Plan multicultural holidays and celebrations.

Ice Breaker: Holiday Opinions   15 minutes

As participants enter the room, give them a copy of the handout "Holiday Opinions." Ask them to complete the five sentences, then find one other person and discuss their answers.

Holiday Opinions

Directions: Complete the following sentences, then share your answers with another person.

1. When I think of holidays, I think of...

   _____

   _____

   _____

   _____

   _____

2. A good celebration should...

   _____

   _____

   _____

   _____

   _____

3. The problem with holidays is...

   _____

   _____

   _____

   _____

   _____

4. If my program changed its policies toward holidays, I would be the most disappointed if...

   _____

   _____

   _____

   _____

   _____

5. In terms of holidays, I would really like it if our program would...

   _____

   _____

   _____

   _____

Four Case Studies: Approaches to
Multicultural Education and Holiday Activities

Case Study One: Christmas Celebrations

You are a child who attends an early childhood program with a long tradition of putting on a Christmas celebration. During the entire month of November, you learn special songs, fingerplays, and a short skit written by your teacher. You are drilled at every free moment: when your class is waiting to use the bathroom, waiting for snack to be served, waiting for the slow kids to finish putting on their coats so you can go outside to play.

Finally the day of the celebration arrives. Your mother makes you wear party clothes even though you wanted to wear sweat pants. She waves her finger at you and says, "Now don't get dirty. And stay away from the paint and markers. I want you to look good at the Christmas celebration."

At day care, the teachers are all tense and preoccupied. Your class spends the morning practicing. You just want to play. Finally, when it is free play time, there are few choices. The teachers say you can look at books, put puzzles together, or play with blocks. The art, dramatic play, and sensory areas are closed because they are too messy and everyone must stay neat and clean.

It's almost time for the celebration. Parents start arriving at school. You see your mom and baby sister. You want to say hi, get a hug from mom, and sit with her. Your teacher holds you back and says, "You can see your mom at the end of the celebration." Your class walks into the gym and stands in front of the parents. You are scared by the flashing lights of cameras and all the strange people. You can't sing because you are so busy watching the people. The little boy next to you starts to cry. You just want to go sit with your mom and have a cookie. (The teacher said that if you sang well you would get a cookie.)

The singing is over. You run to your mom and get a big hug. She says, "You didn't sing. Why didn't you sing? I know you know the words to all of the songs. You sing them all the time for me at home. I don't know what's wrong with you." You ask for a cookie. "All right, but just one," warns your mom.

Now it's time for the parents to go back to work and kids to take naps. You don't want to say good-bye to your mom. You cry and try to hold onto her so she won't leave you. But she says she'll see you later and the teacher picks you up and carries you back into the room. She tells you to go to the bathroom and get on your cot for naptime.

Questions:

1. What were the teachers' goals in planning this celebration?

2. What values are being taught at this celebration?

3. What is the child learning by participating in this celebration?

4. Would you plan a celebration like this one? If so, why? If not, why not?

5. How would you change this celebration to fit with your approach to multicultural education?

Mini-Lecture: Holidays Can Teach Negative and Positive Values

Present a brief lecture on the negative and positive values taught through holidays. Depending on the small group discussions, you may also want to present information on the "holiday craze" in early childhood education and ways to incorporate holidays into a multicultural curriculum. Refer to pages 149 - 152 of *Roots and Wings* in preparing a mini-lecture on this material.

Critical Reflection: Holiday Activities Reflect Approaches to Multicultural Education   30 minutes

Divide the class into small groups of four to six participants. Give each small group a copy of the case studies. Ask them to review the case studies one at a time, with one group member reading the case study aloud, and then answering the questions as a group.

Four Case Studies: Approaches to Multicultural Education and Holiday Activities

Case Study One: Christmas Celebrations

You are a child who attends an early childhood program with a long tradition of putting on a Christmas celebration. During the entire month of November, you learn special songs, fingerplays, and a short skit written by your teacher. You are drilled at every free moment: when your class is waiting to use the bathroom, waiting for snack to be served, waiting for the slow kids to finish putting on their coats so you can go outside to play.

Finally the day of the celebration arrives. Your mother makes you wear party clothes even though you wanted to wear sweat pants. She waves her finger at you and says, "Now don't get dirty. And stay away from the paint and markers. I want you to look good at the Christmas celebration."

At day care, the teachers are all tense and preoccupied. Your class spends the morning practicing. You just want to play. Finally, when it is free play time, there are few choices. The teachers say you can look at books, put puzzles together, or play with blocks. The art, dramatic play, and sensory areas are closed because they are too messy and everyone must stay neat and clean.

It's almost time for the celebration. Parents start arriving at school. You see your mom and baby sister. You want to say hi, get a hug from mom, and sit with her. Your teacher holds you back and says, "You can see your mom at the end of the celebration." Your class walks into the gym and stands in front of the parents. You are scared by the flashing lights of cameras and all the strange people. You can't sing because you are so busy watching the people. The little boy next to you starts to cry. You just want to go sit with your mom and have a cookie. (The teacher said that if you sang well you would get a cookie.)

The singing is over. You run to your mom and get a big hug. She says, "You didn't sing. Why didn't you sing? I know you know the words to all of the songs. You sing them all the time for me at home. I don't know what's wrong with you." You ask for a cookie. "All right, but just one," warns your mom.

Now it's time for the parents to go back to work and kids to take naps. You don't want to say good-bye to your mom. You cry and try to hold onto her so she won't leave you. But she says she'll see you later and the teacher picks you up and carries you back into the room. She tells you to go to the bathroom and get on your cot for naptime.

Questions:

1. What were the teachers' goals in planning this celebration?

2. What values are being taught at this celebration?

3. What is the child learning by participating in this celebration?

4. Would you plan a celebration like this one? If so, why? If not, why not?

5. How would you change this celebration to fit with your approach to multicultural education?

Four Case Studies: Approaches to
Multicultural Education and Holiday Activities

Case Study Two: Winter Celebration

You attend an early childhood program that is known for parent involvement. Tonight you and your family will attend the center's winter celebration. You can't wait till your parents come to pick you up, because that is when the fun begins. While playing in the block area, you feel a tap on your shoulder. It's your dad! "Ready to go?" he asks. He helps you put the blocks away. Your mom and sister are waiting for you at the classroom door. You and your family walk down to the gym, where lots of tables have been set up so that all the families can have dinner together. You show your parents the tablecloths, napkins, and centerpieces you helped decorate.

You sit next to your friend, Marta, and her family. You are too excited to eat much dinner. Your dad takes you and Marta over to where the large motor equipment is set up. You like to climb to the top and slide down the slide. Soon a teacher is calling everyone together. She has a guitar and leads the families in singing some winter songs. Some of the parents don't know the words, so she gives them a piece of paper with the words on it. You sit in mom's lap and sing as loud as you can. You know all the words to the songs. After the singing, people take turns saying what they like about winter. Lots of kids say they like the snow. "Great," says the teacher, "We have lots of snow and winter activities for you tonight." She says you get to choose what you want to do. There are children's movies in the classroom, making snow ice cream in the kitchen, and building a snow castle on the playground. At the tables, people can make bird feeders, sun catchers, snowflakes, hot cocoa mix to take home, or popcorn snowmen.

You want to do it all. But mom says pick one activity for starters. You choose building a snow castle. Mom helps you get bundled up to go outside, and together you join other children and parents in building the castle. Your sister and dad choose to stay inside and make bird feeders. Kids and parents work together to build the castle, and it is completed in no time at all. It's fun to go in and out of the snow castle, and you look forward to playing in it with your friends.

A teacher calls everyone inside. It's almost time to go home. Hot cocoa, apple cider, and cookies are being served in the gym. Dad and sister are waiting with treats for you and mom. A storyteller has come to tell winter bedtime stories. You snuggle up in dad's lap and tell him all about the castle you built. The storyteller tells three winter stories, and then it is time to go home. You feel warm and sleepy inside. Dad helps you put on the snowsuit and carries you out to the car.

Questions:

1. What were the teachers' goals in planning this celebration?

2. What values are being taught at this celebration?

3. What is the child learning by participating in this celebration?

4. Would you plan a celebration like this one? If so, why? If not, why not?

5. How would you change this celebration to fit with your approach to multicultural education?

Four Case Studies: Approaches to
Multicultural Education and Holiday Activities

Case Study Three: Luau

You and your class have been learning about Hawaii. At lunch today, you are having a luau. The teachers make each of you a Hawaiian grass skirt out of crepe paper. The boys get to make construction paper headbands and the girls get to make tissue paper flowers for their hair. When everyone is done, you take off your shoes and put on your Hawaiian costumes. Some children even wore Hawaiian shirts to go with their skirts. Teachers help the boys with their headbands and pin the flowers in the girls' hair. Everyone puts on a flower lei that they made earlier in the week.

Now it's time to walk outside for your luau. Each class enters the luau to the sound of Hawaiian music. You sit on the ground and wait for the teachers to serve you. You eat pineapple and coconuts, sausages, tuna sandwiches, Hawaiian bread, piña colada juice, and banana boats for dessert. You like the tuna sandwich and pineapple best. After lunch, the teachers play Hawaiian records and you dance the hula and do the limbo. You dance silly with your friend, Amber, and your skirt gets torn. There is a contest for the best hula dance, best limbo player, best ukelele player, best rhythm stick player, and best drummer. You win the limbo contest and get a ribbon. You like Hawaiian parties and can't wait to show your mom the blue ribbon.

Questions:

1. What were the teachers' goals in planning this celebration?

2. What values are being taught at this celebration?

3. What is the child learning by participating in this celebration?

4. Would you plan a celebration like this one? If so, why? If not, why not?

5. How would you change this celebration to fit with your approach to multicultural education?

Four Case Studies: Approaches to Multicultural Education and Holiday Activities

Case Study Four: Dr. Martin Luther King Jr.'s Birthday

You attend an early childhood program that celebrates Dr. Martin Luther King, Jr.'s birthday. Before breakfast, the teacher reads you a story about Martin Luther King, Jr. During free play the teacher asks you to come to the art table. She tells you that Martin Luther King, Jr. had a dream that all children would be friends, and asks, "What is your dream for making the world a better place?" She writes your words across the top of the paper. Red, green, and black paints are set out so that you can paint a picture of your dream.

Another teacher is in the dramatic play area helping the children set up chairs and the steering wheel to play the bus boycott. After free play, you and your friends watch a movie about Dr. King and sing songs from the civil rights movement like "We Shall Not Be Moved" and "We Shall Overcome." At the beginning of naptime the teacher plays a tape of Dr. King talking. You listen to his deep, strong voice before falling to sleep. After nap you and your classmates make banners and signs. You have a parade-march around the neighborhood, singing the freedom songs as you walk.

Birthday cake and ice cream is waiting for you when your group returns to the center. At the end of the day your teacher announces that at the end of the week a child will be given a peace prize for being a kind and gentle friend, just like Dr. King was given the Nobel peace prize for his work. You think to yourself, "I'm going to be a good friend."

Questions:

1. What were the teachers' goals in planning this celebration?

2. What values are being taught at this celebration?

3. What is the child learning by participating in this celebration?

4. Would you plan a celebration like this one? If so, why? If not, why not?

5. How would you change this celebration to fit with your approach to multicultural education?

Practical Application: Planning Holiday Celebrations

60 minutes

Mini-Lecture: Guidelines and Ideas for Holidays and Celebrations

Present a mini-lecture on the guidelines for celebrating holidays and ideas for celebrations from pages 153 - 155 in *Roots and Wings*. You may want to make overhead transparencies or handouts of the guidelines and celebration ideas.

Brainstorming: Using the Multicultural Calendar

Refer participants to the calendar section on pages 156 - 157 in *Roots and Wings* and give them an opportunity to briefly review it. Ask the class for their ideas on how they could use this list of dates. Record their ideas on the chalkboard. Encourage and remind participants to integrate a few of these holidays into their curriculum and to avoid overloading the curriculum with holidays and celebrations. If there is time, you may ask if anyone has celebrated any of these holidays in their program and if so, how did they celebrate the holiday with young children?

Planning Holidays and Celebrations

Divide the class into small groups and distribute a copy of the handout "A Variety of Ways to Plan Multicultural Holidays and Celebrations." Ask each group to plan four celebrations, each using a different method. The first celebration will be a combination of similar holidays. The second will be a celebration or holiday to support a multicultural unit theme. (Participants can refer back to pages 73 - 74 in *Roots and Wings* for a list of appropriate unit themes.) The third celebration will be your own unique creation. The last celebration will commemorate the contribution of an important woman or man. Encourage participants to spend about 10 minutes on each celebration.

A Variety of Ways to Plan Multicultural Holidays and Celebrations

1. Combine a number of similar holidays to create one multicultural celebration. How would you celebrate this holiday?

_____

_____

_____

_____

_____

_____

2. Choose one multicultural unit theme. Select a holiday that would compliment and enrich this curriculum unit. How would you celebrate this holiday?

_____

_____

_____

_____

_____

3. Create your own unique celebration for children or children and families. What would you do?

_____

_____

_____

_____

_____

4. Select one hero or shero to commemorate. How would you celebrate this person's life with young children?

_____

_____

_____

_____

_____

Journaling

1. What role do holidays and celebrations play in your program?
2. What changes are you willing to make in how you celebrate holidays with young children?
3. What are you unwilling to change about how you celebrate holidays with young children?

Affirmations

Symbol: sun

1. I use celebrations to bring people together.
2. I integrate holidays and celebrations into the curriculum.
3. I help children and families celebrate our shared humanity.
4. I celebrate life.
5. I celebrate the struggle for peace, justice, and freedom.
6. I respect spiritual beliefs and religious practices of the families I serve.
7. I avoid mimicking religious rites in my classroom.
8. I meet my own needs for tradition by celebrating holidays in my personal life with my family and friends.
9. I create new traditions that all of my children and families can enjoy.
10. I learn about other culture's holidays.

Additional Activities

Plan a Holiday

Ask participants to select one holiday from the calendar section in *Roots and Wings* that they are currently unfamiliar with, research the holiday, and plan a celebration for young children. Participants may want to choose a holiday that is celebrated by one of the families attending their program. Give them the following outline to use as a format in writing the assignment.

Holiday Celebration Planning Form

Name of holiday: _____

Date: _____

Brief description: _____

_____

Activities and events associated with the holiday: _____

_____

_____

_____

_____

Concepts children could learn by being introduced to this holiday: _____

_____

_____

_____

_____

Values that could be taught by teaching children about the holiday: _____

_____

_____

_____

_____

Unit themes that correspond with this holiday: _____

_____

_____

_____

_____

Children's activities: _____

_____

_____

_____

_____

Resources (children's books, films, organizations, people, places): _____

_____

_____

_____

_____

*Note to the instructor: collect, compile, and duplicate the participants' assignments so that each person in the class receives a booklet of holiday activities ideas.

Follow-Up Small Group Discussion

Divide the class into small groups and ask each participant to share her holiday report. Tell the groups to discuss each report by answering the following questions: Which approach to multicultural education does this holiday celebration represent? Do the goals of this celebration seem age-appropriate? If not, how can they be revised so that they are age-appropriate? Are any of the activities stereotypic? If so, which ones? How could the activities be revised to eliminate stereotypes?

Observation

Have participants observe a multicultural celebration in an early childhood classroom. Then ask them to describe the events and the children's behavior. Ask: What are the goals of this celebration? What are the children learning as a result of participating in this celebration? Which approach to multicultural education does this celebration represent? How do you know?

Interview

Lead the class in a brainstorming session around the question, "If you could talk to a person from another culture about holidays and celebrations, what would you want to know?" Ask participants to interview someone from another culture, preferably a parent. Tell them to conduct the interview using the questions generated in class. Set aside time, a week or two later, for participants to share the results of their interviews with one another.

Guest Speaker

Ask a representative from a religious or cultural group to speak to the class. This can be a very helpful experience for teachers who are confused or defensive about holidays and celebrations. A guest speaker can help a class identify religious activities and cultural activities and can provide suggestions for incorporating holidays and celebrations into the curriculum. For example, you may wish to invite a rabbi or staff person from the local Jewish community center, a representative from the Jehovah's Witness church, or a Native American spiritual leader.

What Would You Do?

Distribute a copy of the handout "What Would You Do?" to each participant. Ask them to read through the situations and answer the questions. After 10 - 15 minutes, divide the class into small groups and ask participants to go through each situation and share their responses with one another.

What Would You Do?

Directions: Read through each situation and answer the questions.

1. This year you have a child in your class who is a Jehovah's Witness. In a staff meeting, you ask your fellow teachers for ideas on how to deal with holidays and celebrations in your classroom. One of the teachers says, "Well I'm sure glad she's not in my group because holidays is all we do."

   How would you feel?_____

   _____

   What would you do?_____

   _____

2. You are a teacher in a Head Start program. You are supposed to plan alternative, multicultural celebrations for your classroom, but the parent volunteers want to plan a Christmas party with a tree, Santa Claus, and presents.

   How would you feel?_____

   _____

   What would you do?_____

   _____

3. You teach in a school-age child care program operated by the public schools. Two years ago they eliminated all religious holidays like Christmas and Easter. This year you aren't allowed to celebrate Halloween because it is offensive to some people.

   How would you feel?_____

   _____

   What would you do?_____

   _____

4. The parent advisory committee has ruled that as of this year, your center will no longer celebrate any holidays.

   How would you feel?_____

   _____

   What would you do?_____

   _____

5. You work in a multi-ethnic early childhood program. The director wants to be sensitive to all of the cultural groups and expects you to celebrate all of the traditional holidays along with the major holidays of each culture represented in your program.

   How would you feel?_____

   _____

   What would you do?_____

   _____

What's the Difference?
A Child's Perspective of Race

Description

Get the information you need to create your own developmentally appropriate multicultural activities. Identify how children develop racial attitudes. Discover how developmental theories explain pre-prejudice behavior. Explore the impact of racism on children's development.

Goals

1. Reflect on the development of your own racial awareness.
2. Examine prejudice and how it develops.
3. Identify the physical characteristics young children notice.
4. Identify the stages of racial awareness.
5. Examine how racism impacts children's development.
6. Plan activities that support the development of racial awareness.

Ice Breaker: Memories   15 minutes

Ask participants to find a partner, introduce themselves, and discuss these questions:

1. Think back to when you were a child. When did you first notice people who were racially different from yourself?
2. Did you tell anyone or ask any questions?
3. How did you learn about race?
4. What were you taught about different races?
5. What were you taught about racism?

Bring the group together and introduce the class topic: the development of racial awareness and prejudice in children. Mention that this is an important and yet difficult topic for many adults. I might say something like:

It is impossible to look at children's development of prejudice without reflecting back on our own experiences of noticing differences, being curious about differences, and experiencing adult's responses to these situations. For some of you it will be easy to remember what it was like to be a child. For others, it will be more difficult. Please be patient with yourself if you find it hard to remember. If you find this topic uncomfortable, I ask that you hang in there with me. I too feel vulnerable. But we have to acknowledge, understand, and eliminate prejudice if we are to achieve racial respect, equality, and unity in our country.

Problem Posing: The Hows and Whys of Prejudice   **25 minutes**

Define Terms

Participants may be unfamiliar with or have forgotten the meaning of racism and prejudice. Take a few moments to define these terms. Refer to the definition of terms on pages 18-19 in *Roots and Wings*.

Tell a Story Illustrating Pre-Prejudice in Young Children

Tell one to two stories from your own experience of young children exhibiting pre-prejudice. Ask participants if any of them have similar stories they would like to share with the class. Here is a story that I tell:

I taught in a Euro-American preschool last year. A few of the children in my four-year-old class began playing "Indians." Other than this form of dramatic play, I hadn't overheard the children talking about diversity or noticed any discriminatory behavior. It was early in the year, and I decided to present a multicultural activity that would help me identify the children's level of awareness. I chose an activity called "Pick A Friend" (on page 127 of Roots and Wings*). I brought a stack of photographs of people from a variety of cultures and gave each child four or five pictures to look at and hold. Then I gave each child an opportunity to tell the class who could be their friend and who could not be their friend. Our collection of "friends" was very small.*

Skin color, ugly clothes, and dirty faces or clothes were the main reasons why the people in the photographs couldn't be a friend. I remember one child cocked his head, raised his shoulders, and wrinkled his nose when identifying why a person couldn't be a friend. It was as though he was ashamed to talk about it. Then, two other boys began to giggle. So I asked them to show us their pictures. They showed the class a picture of a Native American woman. She was nicely dressed and was wearing sterling silver earrings. The boys said she couldn't be a friend because she was "…bad and stole the earrings." Then they showed us a picture of an African American toddler. The child was wearing sleeper pajamas and was standing on his tiptoes to see food on the kitchen counter. The children said he couldn't be their friend because he was going to steal the eggs on the kitchen counter. The activity fell apart after that because every time we came to a picture of a person of color, the children said the people in the picture were bad and were going to steal something.

Large Group Discussion

Facilitate a large group discussion around these two questions: How is prejudice formed? Why are children pre-prejudiced? Most participants are likely to identify parents, and you may end up with a lot of parent-blaming. Help participants put the responsibility for prejudice into perspective by identifying and elaborating on the other causes of prejudice. Add any stories you may have of "good" parents whose children showed signs of pre-prejudice, discriminatory behavior, or distorted thinking.

Mini-Lecture: Four Explanations of Pre-Prejudiced Behavior

Present a mini-lecture on the four explanations of pre-prejudiced behavior. Refer to pages 169 - 170 in *Roots and Wings*. Ask participants to think of and share examples for each of the four reasons why children are pre-prejudiced. Distribute the handout "Stereotypes Commonly Accepted by Young Children" as an example of their distorted thinking.

Stereotypes Commonly Accepted by Young Children

Asians and Asian Americans

all look alike

have yellow skin

have slanty eyes and can't see very well

are polite and bow when they greet people

do karate

celebrate exotic festivals

Africans

live in huts and don't wear much clothing

live in the jungle with wild animals

African Americans

have funny hair

get in a lot of fights

all look alike

are mean and scary

Native Americans

take scalps

have red skin

use tepees as houses

speak in grunts

wear feathers and costumes

ride horses

don't live now

Hispanics and Latinos

have only brown hair and brown eyes

are greasy and unclean

have piñatas at all their parties

Adapted from McGinnis, Kathleen, *Cultural Pluralism in Early Childhood Education*.
St. Louis: Parish Board of Education, Missouri Synod, 1986.

Presentation of Content: The Development of Racial Awareness   45 minutes

Brainstorm: What Differences Do Children Notice?

Write the question "What differences do children notice?" on the chalkboard. Ask participants to brainstorm all the human physical characteristics that children notice.

Mini-Lecture: The Development of Racial Awareness

Prepare a mini-lecture on the development of racial awareness in children. Refer to pages 160 - 168 in *Roots and Wings*. You might want to add an introduction to help participants relate this information to multicultural education and what they already know about child development. Say something like:

This is a very important topic for me. Teachers who use a tourist approach to multicultural education often do so out of a desire to provide entertainment and teach children about other cultures. For me, multicultural education is a way to prepare children to live in the United States, which is a multicultural society. As an early childhood educator, I want to focus on the present, and I want to base my teaching practice on a solid understanding of children's development.

Few of us were ever taught about the development of children's racial awareness and the development of prejudice. It isn't in any child development textbooks, and racial awareness is rarely a topic covered in child development or early childhood education courses. It's no surprise then, that many early childhood teachers wonder if children really notice differences, ask if this is a developmentally appropriate topic, and aren't sure how it fits into their understanding of ages and stages.

Racial awareness, racial identity, and the development of prejudice relates to the areas of cognitive, social, emotional, and language development. The development of racial awareness has been studied since the 1940s and 1950s. The research data has been fairly consistent, but more research needs to be done. Here is what we know thus far.

Distribute a copy of the handout "Stages of Racial Awareness" to help participants identify normal steps to a mature understanding and acceptance of racial diversity. Many early childhood teachers have expressed a concern over children labeling and classifying people by color or ethnicity. I believe that this is developmentally appropriate, and if they have an opportunity to label and sort people now, they won't need to later on in life. They will be able to move beyond that point to a more mature level of awareness, such as being able to compare and contrast a minority/majority perspective.

Stages of Racial Awareness

Infants

become aware of self

recognize familiar people and show fear of strangers

recognize and actively explore faces to discover "what is me" and "what is not me"

develop a sense of trust in the world

experience and show fear and anger

Toddlers

identify self as an individual

experience and show shame

are sensitive and "catch" feelings from adults

begin to mimic adult behavior

2s

identify people with words: "me," "mine," "you"

need independence and a sense of control

recognize/explore physical characteristics

ask "What's 'at?"

classify people by gender

learn names of colors

can tell the difference between black and white

may begin to use social labels

may show discomfort around unfamiliar people

3s and 4s

better at noticing differences among people

can identify and match people according to physical characteristics

ask "Why?" questions

no gender, ethnic constancy

susceptible to believing stereotypes

make false associations and overgeneralize

mask fear of differences with avoidance, silliness

5s and 6s

understand cultural identity and enjoy exploring culture of classmates

can identify stereotypes

explore real and pretend, fair and unfair

tend toward rigid thinking and behavior

show aggression through insults and name-calling

Stages of Racial Awareness (cont.)

7s thru 9s

      gender and racial constancy

      understand group membership; form groups to distinguish self from others

      can consider multiple attributes

      aware of racism against own cultural group

      ask "What are you?"

      want and need a wealth of accurate information

      developing personal strength

9s and older

      interested in and aware of world events

      interested in ancestry, history, geography

      understand the terms "ashamed" and "proud"

      can put self in another's shoes

      aware of cultural/political values

      understand racism

      can compare and contrast minority/majority perspective

      can use skills to take social action

After age 9, racial attitudes tend to stay constant
unless the child experiences a life-changing event.
—Frances Aboud

Sources:

Aboud, Frances. *Children and Prejudice*. New York: Basil Blackwill, 1988.

Derman-Sparks, Louise. *Anti-Bias Curriculum*. Washington, DC: NAEYC, 1989.

Derman-Sparks, Louise, Carol Tanaka Higa, Bill Sparks. "Children, Race, and Racism: How Race Awareness Develops," *Interracial Books for Children Bulletin*. Vol.11, No. 3 and 4. New York: Council on Interracial Books for Children, 1989.

Edwards, Carolyn Pope. *Promoting Social and Moral Development in Young Children: Creative Approaches for the Classroom*. New York: Teachers College Press, 1986.

Porter, Judith D.R. *Black Child, White Child: The Development of Racial Attitudes*. Cambridge: Harvard University Press, 1971.

Critical Reflection: How Does Racism Affect Children's Development?

60 minutes

Guided Imagery: Child Inside

This activity will help participants reflect on their own developmental process regarding racial awareness. Prior to this activity you might ask participants to review the stages of racial awareness and identify where they are in their development. I find that many Euro-Americans get "stuck" in the first four years primarily because of the way adults often respond to children's natural curiosity.

Prepare participants for the guided imagery by asking them to relax in their chair, breathe deeply, and close their eyes. You might say something like:

Inside each adult lives the child we once were. Some people call that inner child the "true self" or the "authentic self." I believe that each of us was born an innocent child with a great capacity for having and expressing feeling, a strong desire for intimate relationships, and an insatiable curiosity about the world.

Often adults have long ago "forgotten" their childhood, abandoning the child they once were. This exercise gives you the opportunity to get in touch with your child inside and explore your childhood feelings and thinking related to racial diversity.

Find a comfortable position and let your arms fall loosely at your side with your hands resting in your lap. Close your eyes and begin relaxing your body by taking in slow, deep breaths. If you feel tense or anxious, imagine pushing the tension out of your body each time you exhale.

Then present this guided imagery:

Imagine yourself back in the house or hometown you grew up in. Ask your child inside to come to you. Your child may come to you as a two year old, four year old, or ten year old. It doesn't matter. Just accept and greet the child. Imagine your adult self taking the child by the hand, and allow the child to lead you on a journey into childhood awareness and understanding. Ask the child to remind you about how you developed your racial awareness and understanding. What is it you need to know or remember in order to meet the needs of the children you are teaching? You have three minutes of clock time to think about this.

*

Now prepare to say good-bye to your child inside. Give your child a great big hug. You may want to tell your child that you love her. Thank your child for helping you today and continuing to live on inside you.

*

Take a moment to reflect on what has taken place.

*

When you are ready, open your eyes and join me in this room.

A Dialogue with Your Child Inside

Distribute a piece of paper and a crayon or felt tip marker to each participant. Ask them to take out a pen or pencil. Tell participants they will have a chance to continue the dialogue with their child inside. Ask them to begin a written conversation with their child inside by holding the pen in their dominant hand and the crayon or marker in their nondominant hand. Tell them to use the dominant hand to write questions to their child inside and the nondominant hand to respond.

Here are some sample questions that participants could ask of their child inside. (You may want to write them on the chalkboard.)

1. When were you first aware of race?
2. When did you begin to notice racial differences?
3. How do you feel about racial diversity?
4. What makes you feel this way?
5. How and what did your parents teach you about racial diversity?
6. How did they respond to your comments or questions?
7. What did you need or want from me?
8. How can I help you?

Adapted from a journaling technique developed by Lucia Capacchione, *The Power of Your Other Hand*. North Hollywood, CA: Newcastle Publishing Co., Inc., 1988.

Small Group Discussion: How Does Racism Affect a Child's Development?

Briefly introduce the concept that racism affects children's development. Refer to pages 171 - 175 in *Roots and Wings*. You might want to introduce the concept by posing some questions such as: In thinking about the development of racial awareness in children, what does it matter? How does racial awareness impact a child's development? Divide the class into small groups of four to five participants. Ask the groups to discuss the questions on the handout.

Racism and Development

1. How might denying one's own ethnicity affect growth and development?

2. How might denying other people's race affect a person's growth and development?

3. How might experiencing racial prejudice affect a child's development?

4. How might racial isolation affect a child's development?

5. How might believing one's own race is superior affect a child's development?

6. How might believing one's own race is inferior affect a child's development?

Practical Application: Promoting Racial Awareness
in Children   20 minutes

Ask participants to remain in their small groups. Introduce the idea of planning classroom activities to promote children's development. Ask participants to take out their handout "Stages of Racial Awareness" and select five developmental tasks that they would like to support in their classrooms. Then distribute the handout "Promoting Racial Awareness in Children." Tell participants to record their ideas for supporting children's development on this form. If there is time, ask each group to share their ideas with the class.

Promoting Racial Awareness in Children

Developmental tasks	Activities to support development
1.	1. 2. 3. 4. 5.
2.	1. 2. 3. 4. 5.
3.	1. 2. 3. 4. 5.
4.	1. 2. 3. 4. 5.
5.	1. 2. 3. 4. 5.

Journaling

1. Which stage of racial awareness best describes you?
2. How has growing up in American society influenced your awareness of and attitude toward people who are racially/ethnically different from you?

Affirmations

Symbol: child

1. I recognize that children notice differences.
2. I affirm children's racial identity.
3. I realize ways in which children learn prejudice by growing up in a racist society.
4. I help children accept and trust others.
5. I encourage children to notice the people and objects in their world.
6. I support children's natural curiosity.
7. I welcome children's questions.
8. I provide children with simple, accurate information about race and ethnicity.
9. I help children identify with their ethnic group.
10. I foster ethnic pride in children.
11. I increase my own racial awareness.

Additional Activities

Helping Children Develop Racial Awareness

Use this form to aid participants in promoting racial awareness on an individual basis. Ask participants to identify five children in their classroom, observe the children for a week, record each child's comments and questions, analyze each child's thinking, and identify steps to help the child grow in racial awareness.

Helping Children Develop Racial Awareness

Child's name	Child's comments/ questions	Summary of thinking/ attitudes	Reason for thinking/ attitudes	Steps to help child grow
1.				
2.				
3.				
4.				
5.				

Critical Reflection: Where Do You Stand?

Use this situation as a critical reflection activity. This activity is especially relevant for training directors and people in leadership positions.

Your state legislature is debating the issue of cultural diversity in child care. There has been an increase in racial tension in the junior and senior high schools. Racially motivated crimes are on the rise in the community. Your state has many early childhood programs in place, and the legislators are well aware of the importance of preventing social problems by addressing them in the early years. The legislators are at an impasse due to pressure from four well-meaning groups.

The communities of color want the state to mandate that all providers receive cultural awareness training. They hope that this will lead to more culturally responsive care by teachers (who are predominantly Euro-American). They want the training to include topics such as: awareness of cultural diversity, attitudes about people from other cultures, sensitivity to children's cultural needs, culturally specific child-rearing and family patterns.

The Department of Education, which regulates early childhood programs, is advocating multicultural education in the children's curriculum. They want to see children exposed to other cultures through the teaching materials, learning activities, and holiday celebrations that are all part of the curriculum.

The early childhood professional organizations don't want any new mandates on early childhood teachers. They say that there are enough requirements for teachers as it is, and the state should put its attention and money into raising early childhood teacher salaries.

The family child care providers in the rural communities have contacted their legislators and asked them to vote against any bill, as multicultural education is not an issue of concern or even relevant to their children and families. The last census shows that even though the communities of color have increased in the major metropolitan areas, the rural areas continue to be predominantly Euro-American.

As an early childhood professional, what is your position?

What might be a compromise solution that all groups could agree to?

Identifying Children's Racial Awareness

This activity will help teachers recognize and assess children's racial awareness. Tell participants to prepare an assessment kit that they can use to identify and assess children's racial awareness. Distribute the handout "Make a Racial Awareness Assessment Kit."

Make a Racial Awareness Assessment Kit

Gather the following materials together prior to class: index cards, adult scissors, magazines, construction paper (in a variety of colors), and clear contact paper. Ask participants to bring additional magazines, crayons, and an expandable clasp envelope. Write the directions for making a diagnostic kit on the board for all to see.

A kit should include: 1) drawing paper and crayons, including skin color crayons; 2) a set of 2"x2" construction paper cards in a variety of colors including black, brown, tan, rust, peach, and white; 3) a matching set of pictures of multi-ethnic people; 4) photos of a boy and girl from each ethnic group; 5) interview questions; 6) response forms.

Directions: Put crayons and five sheets of drawing paper into the envelope. Cut out construction paper squares. Cover the squares with clear contact paper to make them more durable. Go through the magazines and find two copies of the same picture. Make sure you have a matching pair of pictures representing each ethnic group. Glue the pictures onto index cards and cover them with clear contact paper. To make the final set of pictures, find a photo of a boy and a girl from each ethnic group. Glue these pictures to index cards and cover them with clear contact paper. Write the interview questions on an index card and pick up five copies of the response form. Put all of the materials in the envelope and label it "Racial Awareness Assessment Kit."

Assessing Children's Racial Attitudes

Interviewing children gives teachers an opportunity to identify children's racial awareness and attitudes. This is not a scientifically proven assessment instrument and should not be used to label children. It is a series of simple open-ended questions that focus on five aspects of racial awareness. Teachers can use the interview questions as an opportunity to raise the issue of race with young children, give children an opportunity to share their thoughts, and to establish a foundation for curriculum planning. Distribute copies of the handout "Racial Awareness Response Form," ask participants to implement it with at least one child, and report the results to the class.

Racial Awareness Response Form

Child_____Birthdate_____

Ethnicity_____Social class_____Gender_____

Tell the child you need help to learn more about what children think. Ask the child, "Could you help me learn about children?" If the child agrees, take the child to a quiet corner in the classroom. Say to the child, "I have some pictures to show you and some questions to ask you. I am going to write down what you say so that I don't forget it."

A. Self-Concept
Lay out the photos of the boys and girls from each ethnic group on a flat surface. Ask the child:

1. "Which one looks like you?"_____

_____

2. "How are you and that child alike?"_____

_____

B. Self-Esteem
Set the drawing paper and crayons out on a hard flat surface in front of the child. Say to the child, "Color a picture of yourself." If the child responds, "I don't know how," say, "Then color a picture of someone who looks like you." Then record:

1. Description of drawing._____

_____

2. Child's comments while drawing._____

_____

C. Racial Awareness and Knowledge of Racial Terms
Mix up the matched set of multi-ethnic people cards. Lay out the photos in front of the child.

1. Ask the child to match the people. If the child has difficulty say, "Can you find

   the other one that is just like this one?" Record comments. _____

_____

2. After the child has matched the pairs, point to each matched set and ask,

   "What do you call these people?"_____

_____

D. Racial Attitude
Show the child the color squares. With each color ask:

1. "What do you think of when you see the color (*name of color*)?"_____

_____

2. "How does the color (*name of color*) make you feel?"_____

_____

Racial Awareness Response Form (cont.)

Show the child the photos of the boys and girls from each ethnic group. Ask the child:

3. "Which one is lazy and stupid?" _____

_____

4. "Which one is mean?" _____

_____

5. "Which one is bad?" _____

_____

6. "Which one is helpful and smart?" _____

_____

7. "Which one is kind?" _____

_____

8. "Which one is good?" _____

_____

9. "Is there anything else you want to tell me about these pictures?" _____

_____

E. Racial Preference

Once again, lay out the card of the multi-ethnic children. Ask the following questions:

1. "Of these children, who could you play with?" _____

_____

2. "Who could be your friend?" _____

_____

3. "Whose house would you like to visit?" _____

_____

4. "Is there anything else you want to tell me about these pictures?" _____

_____

Thank the child for spending time with you and helping you today. Help the child transition back into the classroom activities.

Adapted from   Frances Aboud, *Children and Prejudice.* New York: Basil Blackwell Ltd., 1988.
                Williams and Morland, *Preschool Racial Attitude Measure.* 1976.
                Katz and Zalk, *Katz-Zalk Projective Prejudice Test.* 1978.

Racial Awareness Checklist

Here is yet another format for identifying and assessing children's racial awareness: Ask participants to use the checklist to observe a child in their program. Ask them to bring the completed checklist with them to the next class session. Divide the class into small groups according to the ages of the children observed. For example: everyone who observed a two year old would form a small group, everyone who observed a three year old would form a small group, and so on. Ask participants to present and then compare their findings.

Racial Awareness Checklist

Child _____ Age_____

Social class_____ Gender_____ Birthdate_____

Observer_____ Date_____

_____recognizes familiar people
_____shows fear of strangers
_____trusts others
_____recognizes and identifies self
_____mimics adult behavior
_____identifies people with words like "me," "mine," and "you"
_____recognizes physical characteristics like skin color, hair color
_____describes own physical characteristics
_____asks "What's that?" questions
_____knows names of colors
_____differentiates between the colors black, brown, and white
_____develops attitudes about certain colors
_____uses social labels/terms to describe people
_____notices similarities among people
_____notices differences among people
_____matches people according to their physical characteristics
_____develops attitudes about people based on physical characteristics
_____draws self accurately
_____asks "Why?" questions
_____associates culture with parents and family
_____understands cultural identity
_____demonstrates racial preference
_____identifies stereotypes
_____differentiates between real and pretend
_____differentiates between fair and unfair
_____understands racial constancy
_____understands membership in a cultural group
_____demonstrates positive affiliation with own racial group
_____aware of racism
_____curious about others' ethnicity; asks "What are you?"
_____requests information about own culture
_____requests information about other cultures
_____aware of, interested in world events
_____interested in own ancestry
_____interested in history and geography
_____understands concepts of shame and pride
_____takes another person's perspective
_____aware of cultural values
_____understands racism
_____differentiates between minority and majority perspective
_____associates social action with challenging racism

SESSION TEN

Culturally Responsive Child Care

Description

Develop the sensitivity and perspective that will enable you to provide culturally responsive child care that honors and meets the needs of today's changing families. Get practical tips on how to resolve common classroom conflicts between families and the center.

Goals

1. Recognize that differences between teachers and children, and teachers and families can be a result of cultural differences.
2. Examine how culture influences child-rearing and family patterns.
3. Reflect on your own culture and caregiving style.
4. Examine ways of providing culturally responsive child care.
5. Practice using a problem-solving model to resolve cultural dilemmas.
6. Identify ways to involve families in early childhood programs.

Ice Breaker: The Role of Culture   20 minutes

Ask participants to find three other people and form a small group. Tell them to introduce themselves and answer these questions. Give each group a large sheet of paper and ask them to record their answer to the third question.

1. What is culture?
2. What role does culture/ethnicity play in your own life?
3. What are the values of Euro-American culture (white folks)? Write your definition on the large piece of paper.

Note to instructor: If you are presenting this material as a single workshop session, you may want to begin with a more in-depth discussion on culture. Ask participants to brainstorm the things (objects), customs (how people live their daily lives), and values (beliefs, reasons for actions) that are culturally-related. Look on page 22 in *Roots and Wings* for an example of this exercise.

Collect the lists of Euro-American values and tape them to the wall so that everyone can see them. Review the lists with the class and comment on the activity. You might say:

I'd like to begin by asking you to think about the role of culture in your life and about Euro-American values, because often Euro-Americans lack cultural awareness. Ask a white person, for example, "What does it mean to be white?" and the most common response is, "I don't know. I've never really thought about it."

This absence of a cultural identity is a result of at least two dynamics. First, the strong belief in the melting pot (that everyone is the same) which creates a denial of culture. Second, that Euro-Americans are the dominant culture, which results in assuming that their ways are the norm.

If we are to provide culturally responsive child care, we must first recognize Euro-American culture and begin to identify the ways that current child-rearing beliefs and styles are influenced by culture. It is my belief that as long as early childhood teachers are ignorant of the role culture plays in child-rearing, they will likely assume that their caregiving style is the norm, expect all parents to implement their caregiving style, and negatively judge families that follow different child-rearing patterns.

Problem Posing: How Do Cultural Differences Create Classroom Dilemmas?   20 minutes

Visualization

Read the following situation to the class. Ask participants to sit quietly and, as they listen, imagine they are the baby in this situation.

You are an 8-month-old infant. You have lived your life in an apartment shared with your parents, grandparents, and older brothers and sisters. At night you sleep in your parents' bed, snuggled up between them. All day long you are held by your mom. Sometimes she holds you in her arms, but most of the time she puts you in a cloth sling that holds you close to her body. You like it there because it is safe and warm. You also enjoy being held by the other members of your family. Your sister likes to carry you around and bounce you in the air and your brother sticks out his tongue and makes silly faces that make you laugh.

*

One day, you and mom go to a place called a child care center. Mom takes you out of the sling and hands you over to another woman. You look around, and mom is smiling and waving bye-bye. You reach out for her, but she is gone. You do not know this new person. She looks funny, smells funny, talks funny, and holds you differently than anyone else. You cry and cry. She takes out a blanket and lays it on the floor. She puts some toys on the blanket. Then she lays you on the floor and tells you to play with the toys. You look up at her and start to cry some more. Everything looks different, you don't know what to do with the toys, and right now you don't care about the toys.

*

A woman with a smiling face walks over to you and picks you up. It feels good to be in someone's arms again. She says, "I bet you're hungry. Let's see if you'd like a bottle." She sits you in a hard plastic box and puts a piece of rubber in your mouth. You shake your head and spit it out. You kick and squirm, trying to get out of the box, and you cry when the smiling face tries to put the rubber in your mouth. She gives up and carries you to a dark room. She says, "Maybe you are tired and would like to take a nap. I'll bet you'll feel better after you sleep for awhile." Now you are in a different kind of box. It has very high rails. You cannot get out and you are all alone in the dark. You are tired of crying and fall asleep.

Large Group Discussion

As a large group, discuss the situation. Ask these questions: How would you feel if you were this baby? How would you feel if you were this baby's caregiver? What role does culture play in this caregiver-infant relationship? List participants' answers on the chalkboard to this last question: How do cultural differences create dilemmas in the classroom?

Presentation of Content: Culture, Families, and the Classroom   60 minutes

Mini-Lecture: Families and Culture

Present a lecture on the role of culture in families. Refer to pages 178 - 180 in *Roots and Wings*. A lecture could include a definition of family; the myth that the nuclear family is the normal, healthy family; different family structures; enculturation; and how cultural values within a family change.

Small Groups: Ways and Means: Associating Culture with Child-Rearing Patterns

Divide the class into small groups and distribute a copy of the handout "Ways and Means: Associating Culture with Child-Rearing Patterns." Ask them to identify the current approach among early childhood teachers in America for each element of child-rearing listed. You may want to use the National Association for the Education of Young Children's (NAEYC) *Developmentally Appropriate Practice* as a resource for identifying current Euro-American thinking regarding child-rearing.

Ways and Means: Associating Culture with Child-Rearing Patterns

Directions: Use this handout to help you identify current Euro-American thinking regarding child-rearing. Consider three sources when answering the questions: 1) developmentally appropriate practice; 2) early childhood textbooks and information you have received in workshops; 3) your program's policies and procedures.

What are the age-related expectations?

infants:	age _____	
	expectation _____	
toddlers:	age _____	
	expectation _____	
preschoolers:	age _____	
	expectation _____	
schoolagers:	age _____	
	expectation _____	

How important is it that children acquire these age-related skills?_____

_____

What is the sleep pattern of young children in your program? _____

_____

How do you put children down for a nap?_____

_____

What type of foods do you serve at meals? _____

_____

How do you organize and serve meals? _____

_____

What are children's responsibilities in the classroom?_____

_____

How do you toilet train children? _____

_____

How do you discipline children? _____

_____

What values do you try to instill in children? _____

_____

Reading: Culture and the Classroom

Ask participants to read pages 181-186 in *Roots and Wings* to gain an understanding of how culturally based family patterns may influence the classroom.

Critical Reflection: Am I Culturally Responsive?   35 minutes

Large Group Discussion

Facilitate a large group discussion on the role of the dominant culture in child care. Consider using these questions to start the discussion: How do centers force the dominant culture onto all their children and families? How can a center be more like a home? What rules/policies would you need to break in order to provide culturally responsive care? What rules/policies could you design to ensure culturally responsive care?

Guided Imagery: Increasing "Response-Ability"

Ask participants to find a comfortable sitting position, rotate their shoulders a few times so that their arms hang loosely at their side, and hands rest in their lap. Say:

Close your eyes and breathe slowly and deeply. Now is the time to reflect on yourself as a caregiver of children. As a professional caregiver you are responsible for many children at a time. Imagine yourself surrounded by a group of young children. Every culture, race, and economic class is represented in this group. Now imagine the parents of these children joining their child. Some stand behind their children holding hands or with their hands on the child's shoulders. Others hold their child in their arms. Some children are at their parent's side, holding on to the parent's coat leg or dress hem. You are still at the center of the group and these people, these parents and children, are looking to you to teach and care for their child.

*

Notice your mind. Examine your thoughts, attitudes, and beliefs. In what ways are you rigid, defensive, or closed to these parents and children? Do you struggle with arrogance, thinking that you know more or what is best for these children than their parents do? Are you ignorant—ignoring the role that culture and social class plays in the lives of these people? Are you overcome by self-protection and self-interest? Is your mind saying, "I want it my way. This is how I do it in my classroom." Notice the rigid, defensive, protective stance in the face of diversity.

*

Imagine yourself softening. You are like a drawing with bold colors and strong dark lines that turns into a watercolor painting. The colors soften and merge with one another, making the images appear less distinct and separate from one another.

*

Allow yourself to open up to cultural diversity. Your mind comes to understand the importance of culture to child-rearing. You perceive the complexity of each of the family's lives. Your heart opens to each family and child. You are able to embrace the challenge of providing culturally responsive child care.

*

Find your soft spot. Focus on the place inside of you that feels compassion and affection for others. Imagine your compassion is like a flower bud that opens to a full bloom under the warmth of the sun. Let yourself feel and be full of acceptance... trust...honesty...affection...support...confidence...cooperation...compromise... unity.

*

Imagine yourself greeting, engaging, and embracing the children and families that encircle you. You are open and relaxed. You listen without judging. They teach you about their child. You model their style of caregiving. You use the sense of touch to reach out and connect with them. You feel warm, confident, and strong as a result of creating unity from diversity.

*

Accept and create within yourself response-ability. If you can, imagine yourself welcoming diversity and creating respectful, honest, and supportive relationships with children and families. Know that whatever you can imagine, you can create. Whatever you believe in you will learn how to do. When you are ready, open your eyes and join me in this room.

Self-Examination: What If?

Tell participants that the importance of this activity is to allow yourself to think about alternatives and the consequences of change. Distribute a copy of the handout "What If?" to each participant. Tell them this exercise will help them identify which caregiving behaviors would be easiest to change and which would be the most difficult, given their situation.

As an instructor, look for areas of rigid thinking, such as when a participant might say, "We could never do that." Bring these situations to a large group discussion and attempt to uncover the thinking or feelings behind the rigidity. Wrap up the activity by commenting on the fact that our world does not fall apart as a result of these and or other changes, and that gradual changes result in transforming a monocultural or Euro-centric program into a multicultural program.

What If?

This activity allows you to think about diversifying caregiving routines and procedures. Read through the list and…

1. Circle those practices that would be the easiest to change.
2. Put a star next to those practices that you could never do.
3. Underline those practices that would be the most difficult to change.

What would happen if we considered different family systems in the design of an early childhood program?

What if we created mixed-age groups?

What if we allowed siblings to stay together during the day?

What if we allowed a child to visit his baby sister?

What would happen if we respected the power structure of various families?

What if we allowed the children to participate in making the classroom rules?

What if we invited the child's mother and grandmother to the parent/teacher conference?

What would happen if we respected how parents work and how social status influences their parenting?

What if we allowed the children to move around more/be more physically active during free-choice play?

What if we included some product-oriented activities in the curriculum?

What if we granted parents' requests that their child not go outside today?

What would happen if we considered parents' attitudes toward teachers?

What if the children were to call me by my first name?

What if the children were to use a title of respect to identify me?

What would happen if we recognized that child development theories and developmentally appropriate practices are culturally based?

What if we held a baby instead of putting her on the floor?

What if we allowed parents to decide when their child is ready to be toilet trained?

What if we allowed toddlers to have bottles, pacifiers, or blankets?

What If? (cont.)

What would happen if we incorporated values from different cultures into our program?

What if we played touching and "people" games with babies instead of encouraging them to play with toys and objects?

What if we allowed children to bring toys from home?

What if we didn't make children share?

What if we didn't make all children be here by 9:00 a.m.?

What if we washed children's faces, combed their hair, and tucked in their shirts toward the end of the day?

What if we modeled different styles of communication?

What if we casually told stories throughout the day to make a point or teach a concept?

What if we allowed children to show their anger?

What if we recognized that some parents choose child discipline methods that are part of their culture?

What if we tried humor and gentle harassment with some children?

What if we lowered our voice and talked very softly when disciplining some children?

What if we used "if…then…" statements with some children?

Add your own what ifs…

_____

_____

_____

_____

_____

_____

_____

_____

_____

_____

_____

Practical Application: Resolving Classroom Dilemmas and Involving Parents 60 minutes

Small Group: Resolving Classroom Dilemmas

Divide the class into small groups of three or four. Distribute and review the handout "Resolving Classroom Dilemmas." Ask each group to choose one culturally-related classroom dilemma and go through the steps listed on the handout to resolve the situation. After fifteen minutes, bring the class together and give each group an opportunity to share how they would resolve their dilemma.

Resolving Classroom Dilemmas

1. **Analyze the situation** and identify ways in which you may be involved in a cultural dilemma. Ask yourself:

    What is the child's experience at home?

    How is the child's experience related to a cultural practice or value?

2. **Don't blame the child.** The child is not bad, evil, spoiled, or developmentally delayed. Contrary to how it may seem, the child is not out to get you. The child may be acting in a culturally appropriate way.

3. **Get information.** Read through the child's file. Talk to the child's parents. Ask the parents what they would do in this situation.

4. **Realize the child can't cope.** The child is responding to a new situation in the only way he knows how.

5. **Respond to the child and parents as individuals.** Be willing to bend, revise, and change in order to meet their needs.

Mini-Lecture: Early Childhood Programs as Extended Family

Present a brief lecture on the importance of early childhood programs serving as extended family in order to provide complimentary care. Refer to pages 188 - 189 in *Roots and Wings*.

Small Group: Involving Families in Your Program

Tell participants you want to give them a chance to generate ideas for making programs more culturally responsive. Briefly describe each of the program elements that relate to parent involvement and culturally responsive child care:

> Enrollment Meeting
>
> Enrollment Form
>
> Home Visits
>
> Daily and On-Going Communication/Newsletters
>
> Curriculum and Classroom Events

Form small groups around each of the preceding topics and give participants a choice of which small group they would like to join. Ask each group to identify how their program element can be used to increase parent involvement and make the program more culturally responsive.

Journaling

1. How did your ancestors come to America? Why did they come? What were their hopes and fears? Did they come alone or with other family members? Did they long to return to their homeland?
2. What do you need to feel accepted and valued as a person?
3. What changes can you make in your classroom (or entire program) to provide care and early education that is culturally responsive to the families you serve?

Affirmations

Symbol: heart

1. I establish and maintain positive parent-teacher relations.
2. I communicate honestly with parents.
3. I cooperate and compromise with parents.
4. I release my negative expectations of parents.
5. I let go of my belief in one right way of child-rearing.
6. I recognize and understand the complexity of children's lives.
7. I recognize the ways in which an early childhood program is a cultural setting.
8. I explore the role of culture in my own family and style of child-rearing.
9. I open myself to learning from other cultures.
10. I look for the strengths in each family.
11. I help families maintain and pass on their culture to their children.
12. I let go of expecting all families to share my values and parenting style.
13. I bend and flex to meet the needs of each child in my room.

Additional Activities

Taking Action

Ask participants to complete this assignment on their own and report back to the class at a later date. Distribute a copy of the handout "Taking Action to Implement Culturally Responsive Child Care." Some participants may have difficulty thinking of a way to take action. If this is the case, take a moment to brainstorm options as a large group when giving this assignment.

Taking Action to Implement
Culturally Responsive Child Care

1. Choose one thing you can do toward providing culturally responsive child care.

   _____

2. Describe what you will do.

   _____

   _____

   _____

3. List the steps in the order you will take them.

   _____

   _____

   _____

   _____

   _____

   _____

Answer these questions after you have taken action.

1. What happened? How did others respond?

   _____

   _____

   _____

2. What do you think? How do you feel?

   _____

   _____

   _____

3. Evaluate the action step. Was it useful? Was it worth it? Did it help? Did it hurt anyone?

   _____

   _____

   _____

4. Would you do it differently next time? If so, what changes would you make?

   _____

   _____

   _____

Assess Your Cultural Response-Ability

The handout "How's My Cultural Response-Ability?" is the most confrontive activity in this book. Its purpose is to make teachers sit up and pay attention. Use this self-assessment tool to help participants reflect on their cultural awareness and openness to individualizing care.

Thinking and talking about cultural responsiveness is exclusive of practicing cultural sensitivity. Unfortunately, many teachers attend a training session or a series of sessions on multicultural education, appear to be in full agreement, and talk as though they implement it. But once I start talking about culturally responsive care, I notice participants' backs stiffen, faces frown, and heads shake from side to side. Rapid-fire questions come with an accusatory tone, "Are you saying…," "Do you mean you're telling me…," "Do you really expect…," "So I'm supposed to…"

Needless to say, "Assess Your Cultural Response-Ability" is neither an ice breaker nor a closing activity. It requires substantial preparation by creating a context in which cultural responsibility can be examined. The activity works best when there is a break between sessions because it throws participants into cognitive dissonance and they need time for accommodating the material. "Assess Your Cultural Response-Ability" always requires some follow-up discussion. Expect a heated debate and try to get participants to discuss: the role of personality, temperament and culture as sources of uniqueness, the meaning of individualized care, the inability of one caregiving method/style to meet everyone's needs, and the importance of flexible center policies and procedures.

How's My Cultural "Response-Ability?"

1. When a two-and-a-half-year-old boy moves up to your classroom, still carrying around a baby bottle, you persuade him to give it up.

   | |_____| |_____| |_____| |_____| |
   strongly agree   agree   neutral   disagree   strongly disagree

2. You accept Mitsuye's continuous crying and try to soothe her. Her family recently arrived from Japan and she has never been cared for by someone other than her mother.

   | |_____| |_____| |_____| |_____| |
   strongly agree   agree   neutral   disagree   strongly disagree

3. As an infant teacher, you expect all babies to be able to play with toys on the floor.

   | |_____| |_____| |_____| |_____| |
   strongly agree   agree   neutral   disagree   strongly disagree

4. You are careful about how you guide Lloyd's behavior. His mother has told you that he doesn't respond well to direct confrontations and is likely to ignore you or fall limp to the floor.

   | |_____| |_____| |_____| |_____| |
   strongly agree   agree   neutral   disagree   strongly disagree

5. You are shocked and appalled that Charrika's mother sends her to school without wearing underwear.

   | |_____| |_____| |_____| |_____| |
   strongly agree   agree   neutral   disagree   strongly disagree

6. You watch Brent carefully when he plays in the sandbox because you understand how difficult it is to get sand out of his curly hair.

   | |_____| |_____| |_____| |_____| |
   strongly agree   agree   neutral   disagree   strongly disagree

7. You think Carmen's parents could care less about her because they don't keep an extra change of clothes for her at the center.

   | |_____| |_____| |_____| |_____| |
   strongly agree   agree   neutral   disagree   strongly disagree

8. You ask Bettina's parents to make you a cassette tape of the music they listen to at home. Now you play the tape during the day while the children are playing.

   | |_____| |_____| |_____| |_____| |
   strongly agree   agree   neutral   disagree   strongly disagree

9. You give Tawnya, the only African American child enrolled in your program, extra attention because she is so cute.

   | |_____| |_____| |_____| |_____| |
   strongly agree   agree   neutral   disagree   strongly disagree

10. Next week Che will join your class. Tomorrow you will meet with his parents to learn more about his family.

|_____|_____|_____|_____|
strongly agree · · · · · agree · · · · · neutral · · · · · disagree · · · · · strongly disagree

11. Anya's dad is large and speaks with an accent that makes it difficult for you to understand him. You try to avoid talking to him.

|_____|_____|_____|_____|
strongly agree · · · · · agree · · · · · neutral · · · · · disagree · · · · · strongly disagree

12. You avoid patting Ter on the head because it is culturally disrespectful.

|_____|_____|_____|_____|
strongly agree · · · · · agree · · · · · neutral · · · · · disagree · · · · · strongly disagree

13. You can't believe it, no matter how many times you tell Becca's grandfather that school starts at 9:00, he continues to bring her between 9:30 and 10:00.

|_____|_____|_____|_____|
strongly agree · · · · · agree · · · · · neutral · · · · · disagree · · · · · strongly disagree

14. You have noticed that Rajne eats a lot of sweets and snack foods at school. You call his mom to talk about the lunches he brings to school.

|_____|_____|_____|_____|
strongly agree · · · · · agree · · · · · neutral · · · · · disagree · · · · · strongly disagree

15. You feel sorry for Carlos and Antonio. They seem to have a difficult time adjusting to your day care, and you feel like there isn't anything you can do that will help.

|_____|_____|_____|_____|
strongly agree · · · · · agree · · · · · neutral · · · · · disagree · · · · · strongly disagree

16. You usually don't rock infants when putting them down for nap because you want them to learn how to go to sleep by themselves. But, after meeting with Lee's mom, you have agreed to rock her to sleep.

|_____|_____|_____|_____|
strongly agree · · · · · agree · · · · · neutral · · · · · disagree · · · · · strongly disagree

17. You are worried that Jean-Paul won't be successful when he starts school unless his parents start speaking English at home.

|_____|_____|_____|_____|
strongly agree · · · · · agree · · · · · neutral · · · · · disagree · · · · · strongly disagree

18. You recognize how important it is to Camille that her infant daughter, Chidi, and her preschool-age son, Elton, are together. You arrange for Elton to spend time each day playing with his sister in the infant room.

|_____|_____|_____|_____|
strongly agree · · · · · agree · · · · · neutral · · · · · disagree · · · · · strongly disagree

19. You expect all of the four-year-olds to sit still and listen during circle time.

    I_____I_____I_____I_____I
    strongly agree   agree   neutral   disagree   strongly disagree

20. You help Fabrizio become bilingual by labeling the shelves and interest areas in both Italian and English.

    I_____I_____I_____I_____I
    strongly agree   agree   neutral   disagree   strongly disagree

21. Socorro comes to school in party dresses. Her mother has complained that Socorro gets so dirty at school and has asked you to make sure she doesn't get paint all over her clothes. You believe that messy art experiences are essential for creative and sensory development, and refuse to discourage a child from participating in these key activities, no matter what parents say.

    I_____I_____I_____I_____I
    strongly agree   agree   neutral   disagree   strongly disagree

22. Miriam is not allowed to eat certain foods. You check the menu ahead of time to make sure she always has an acceptable alternate.

    I_____I_____I_____I_____I
    strongly agree   agree   neutral   disagree   strongly disagree

23. It really bugs you that Kimong doesn't talk more. You try to find a way to make her open up.

    I_____I_____I_____I_____I
    strongly agree   agree   neutral   disagree   strongly disagree

24. Tia says she hates all police officers. You ask her parents for advice and figure out what to do.

    I_____I_____I_____I_____I
    strongly agree   agree   neutral   disagree   strongly disagree

25. You ask the director to terminate Andrew because he cries all the time and doesn't understand a word of English. You and your aide are having to spend too much of your time with him.

    I_____I_____I_____I_____I
    strongly agree   agree   neutral   disagree   strongly disagree

Scoring

For each of the odd-numbered questions give yourself a…

0   if your circled strongly agree
1   if you circled agree
2   if you circled neutral
3   if you circled disagree
4   if you circled strongly disagree

For each of the even numbered questions give yourself a...
   4   if you circled strongly agree
   3   if you circled agree
   2   if you circled neutral
   1   if you circled disagree
   0   if you circled strongly disagree

Tally your points below

1. _____	14. _____
2. _____	15. _____
3. _____	16. _____
4. _____	17. _____
5. _____	18. _____
6. _____	19. _____
7. _____	20. _____
8. _____	21. _____
9. _____	22. _____
10. _____	23. _____
11. _____	24. _____
12. _____	25. _____
13. _____	

TOTAL_____

Interpreting Your Score

90 - 100 Culturally Responsive.
   You probably see children within their family and social context. You are willing to flex and bend to provide culturally responsive child care. You put positive energy into solving or managing problems. You are able to individualize caregiving routines and your caregiving style.

80 - 89 Culturally Aware.
   You probably realize that culture plays a role in children's behavior and family patterns. As you learn more about how culture influences child-rearing, you begin to incorporate this knowledge into your caregiving and relationships with parents. You have a good start. Try to build on it by working with one child at a time.

70 - 79 It's a personality clash.
   You might be thinking that differences in parenting styles and expectations are related to personality rather than cultural patterns. Perhaps you didn't realize that culture plays an important role in the daily lives of children and families. Improve your cultural response-ability by reviewing Chapter 8 in *Roots and Wings*. Choose a problem situation and think about it from a cultural perspective. Try to resolve the situation using the steps for resolving cultural dilemmas in *Roots and Wings*. Also, review the list of attitudes at the bottom of this page. Try to demonstrate the positive attitudes when you are working with children.

How's My Cultural "Response-Ability?" (cont.)

60- 69 My way is best.

You might have a tendency to think that you know what is best for children. It might be because you haven't had much exposure to cultural differences and think that all families parent the same way. Having a sense of superiority can prevent you from accepting and affirming the strengths of others. Try to shift the focus from yourself and how you were parented to observing and learning how other parents raise children. Also try to develop the ability to decenter and take another person's perspective. Try putting yourself in a parent's shoes and really view the situation from their perspective. Really work on being open and flexible.

Below 60 Different is bad.

You might really be afraid of differences. Try to be aware of how often you try to avoid differences. Sometimes caregivers who are afraid of differences believe in treating all children the same. Try making a list of all the bad things that will happen if you were to treat a child as an individual. Then do the opposite—treat the child as an individual and see what happens! Review Chapter 8 in *Roots and Wings* and examine your need for control. Do you believe that you will be in control if everyone is the same, doing the same thing? Are you afraid that the situation will become chaotic or unmanageable if people are different and are parenting differently? Try to believe that differences are good and that differences give us strength and richness.

Each question in this self-test measures a personal attitude that is important to culturally responsive caregiving. The attitudes are listed below, alongside the question number.

1. coercion, manipulation	14. honesty
2. patience	15. powerlessness
3. ignorance	16. flexibility, compromise
4. trust	17. cynicism
5. arrogance	18. unity, continuity
6. knowledge and understanding	19. rigidity
7. blame	20. support
8. cooperation	21. self-interest
9. guilt	22. respect
10. willingness	23. control
11. fear	24. intuitive problem solving
12. cultural awareness	25. efficiency
13. frustration	

Debate

Debates help teachers realize that there are at least two perspectives on an issue. Culturally responsive child care is an issue that lends itself to a debate. Some parents believe that their children are best served by caregivers or programs within their cultural community. For example, African American children would attend Afro-centric programs, Jewish children attend a Jewish program and so on. Another perspective of some parents is that multicultural programs are more beneficial to their children.

Divide the class into four small groups: minority parents who believe in monocultural child care/early education, Euro-American parents who believe in monocultural child care/early education, minority parents who believe in multicultural child care/early education, Euro-American parents who believe in multicultural child care/early education. Ask each small group to prepare arguments for their position and against the other position.

Once arguments and positions have been identified, combine the two small groups that share the same position into one group, so that the class is divided into two groups. Introduce the debate format and give the two groups time to make final preparations.

Each group will have five minutes to present their position and two minutes for rebuttal. Repeat the presentation - rebuttal sequence. End the debate with each side taking two minutes for closing remarks. Immediately follow up the debate with a large group discussion to acknowledge the ways in which debates can polarize and identify strategies to negotiate a resolution to the issues.

Interview

Ask participants to interview a parent from a culture different from their own. As a large group, have the class identify questions to be asked in the interview. Create an interview form from their questions, duplicate the interview form, and distribute it to each participant. Ask participants to share their results with the class. You may want to discuss the importance of anonymity in collecting this type of information. Ask participants to either use the subject's first initial or change their name when recording and reporting the interview.

Panel Discussion

Organize a panel of representatives from the communities of color in your community. Try to find people with a strong cultural identity who are parents and have utilized some form of child care, or someone who is familiar with child care, and early childhood education.

Help the class prepare to question the panel by asking them, "What questions would you ask if you could talk with a parent from another culture about family, parenting, child-rearing, or early childhood education ?" List the questions on the chalkboard or a sheet of chart paper. Also sensitize them to the panel members. It is very difficult to talk to a group of people, especially if you are a person of color talking before a group of Euro-Americans. I ask that you respect these people and do not ask them to speak on behalf of their entire culture. Ask them questions as individuals.

Begin the panel by asking the members to introduce themselves. You may want to ask them a few general questions such as: Please describe your family; what type of child care arrangements have you used? Which type of child care do you prefer? What do you look for in a child care provider/early childhood teacher? Then ask the panel members to answer the participants' questions. Leave some time at the end for a few questions from the class and final comments from the panel members.

Be prepared to restate participants' questions or ask a participant to restate her question. Class participants will often ask questions that put panel members in a position of speaking on behalf of their entire culture. As the instructor, you will need to take an active role to protect the panel members. End the panel by summarizing the discussion and thanking the panel members for their willingness to participate.

Follow-up the panel with small group discussions. Give each group a sheet of chart paper and ask them to make a mind map/word web of the themes that they heard in the panel.

Questions for Further Discussion
1. When is a family characteristic cultural and when is it a result of poverty and oppression?
2. Is there a difference between culturally responsive child care and high quality individualized care? If so, what is it?
3. Is developmentally appropriate practice Euro-centric? Is it appropriate for everyone? For example, does it name high quality African American child care?

Talking to Children about Differences

Description

Talking to children about diversity can be difficult. Increase your comfort level by learning how to expand children's distorted thinking, answer children's questions, and challenge their discriminatory behavior.

Goals

1. Recognize the power of words.
2. Examine the consequences of silence.
3. Identify how to empower children through language.
4. Practice using words to expand children's thinking.
5. Practice responding to children's questions.
6. Practice responding to children's discriminatory behavior.

Ice Breaker: What's in a Word?   20 minutes

Play a Game: What's That Saying?

Play a version of a popular television game show in which contestants try to correctly identify a saying, name of a person or place by spinning a prize wheel and selecting the alphabet letters. Prepare for the activity by making a spinner and writing the saying on cards. To make the spinner, copy the spinner pattern below and glue it onto a 3" x 3" piece of oak tag. Cut the arrow out of oak tag and attach it to the spinner with a paper fastener. Write each letter of the following saying on a piece of oak tag or poster board:

Sticks and stones may break my bones
but names can never hurt me.

To play the game, tape the letters on the board or a blank wall. Leave a space between the words. Tell the participants that the object of the game is to guess the saying that relates to this session's topic. Give each of the participants an opportunity to spin and guess a letter. Participants may only guess the saying when it is their turn. You may want to have a gag gift handy for the winner.

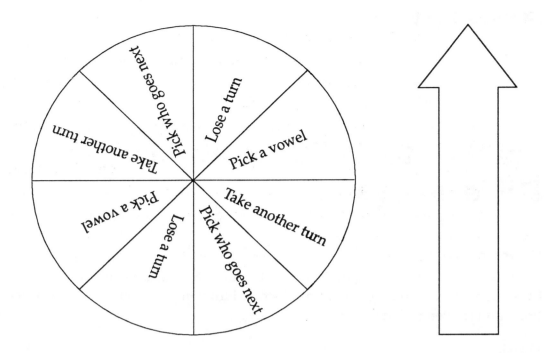

Small Group Discussion: Did Names Hurt You?

Ask participants to form small groups of three to four and answer these questions: What names did your siblings, classmates, and friends call you when you were a child? How did you feel when kids called you these names? Do you agree or disagree with the saying? Why or why not?

Problem Posing: Words Discriminate and Words Empower   30 minutes

Large Group Discussion

Introduce the concept that words are powerful tools, both for hurting others and for empowering others. Pose these two questions: How does language perpetuate discrimination? How can language eliminate prejudice?

Small Group Project

Distribute a copy of the handout "What's in a Word?" Ask participants to rejoin their small groups and use the handout to identify how words can be tools of empowerment or discrimination. Bring the class back together and ask each group to share their words with the rest of the class. You may want to have your own list of words (one is included below but add your own words) to use as examples in case the participants get stuck on one of the questions and can't identify any examples of their own.

What's in a Word:

1. Nigger, Polack, Leper, Chink, Spic, Wetback
2. Nonwhite, non-English speaking, minority, white privilege, racial equality
3. Pure as the driven snow, white lie, white collar worker, white gold, white hope, white house, white paper, white tie affair
4. Black as sin, black lie, black heart, black list, black mail, call the kettle black, black market, black sheep, black mark
5. We're all the same, color blind, selective ignorance, assimilation, melting pot
6. Black is beautiful, indigenous people, first nations
7. Racial insensitivity, culturally invasive, demoralization, complementarily, bigot
8. Personal responsibility, white flight, white guilt, white privilege

What's in a Word?

Directions: List as many words as you can for each of the following categories.

1. Slang words that devalue or defame people because of their culture.

   _____

   _____

   _____

2. Words that assume that Euro-Americans (white folks) are the norm.

   _____

   _____

   _____

3. Words or phrases that describe something that is white in positive terms. Example: white knight.

   _____

   _____

   _____

4. Words or phrases that describe something that is black in negative terms. Example: black hole.

   _____

   _____

   _____

5. Words or phrases that deny or ignore cultural diversity.

   _____

   _____

   _____

6. Words or phrases that empower people of color.

   _____

   _____

   _____

7. Words or phrases that help people change their prejudiced thinking or behavior.

   _____

   _____

   _____

8. Words or phrases that help Euro-Americans recognize their role in a racist society.

   _____

   _____

   _____

Codification: The Power of Silence

Display the quote by Pastor Niemoller (page 196 in *Roots and Wings*) by making an overhead transparency or writing the quote on a piece of chart paper and taping it to a wall. Ask participants to read the quote. Use the quote to help participants name their problems with silence and identify the root causes of choosing silence as a response to discrimination and oppression. Pose questions like: How does this quote relate to teaching multicultural education? When have you been silent? When have you experienced someone else's silence? What is the result of silence? What are some ways we can respond other than silence?

Presentation of Content: Empowering Children through Language   45 minutes

Mini-Lecture: Creating a Place of Empowerment

Prepare a mini-lecture on empowering children through language. Refer to pages 198 - 200 in *Roots and Wings*. Make sure that you address accepting cultural dialects and native languages, teaching children to use their words to express feelings, and helping children expand their thinking. Depending on the participants and their concerns, you may want to present additional material on ways to incorporate other languages into the classroom or focus more on basic communication skills.

Case Studies: Helping Children Expand Their Thinking

Lead the class through two or three case studies. Use the situations provided, your own, or ask participants to share one of their own experiences of a child exhibiting distorted thinking. Present the case study situation and have the class brainstorm ways the child's teacher could expand the child's thinking by paying close attention, setting a calm and relaxed atmosphere, affirming the child's thinking, clarifying the child's thinking, and offering thought-provoking comments.

Situation 1: A Euro-American child says, "I'm white. I don't have a color."

Situation 2: An African American child looks at her Asian American classmate and says, "She got them funny eyes. I bet she can't even see out of them eyes."

Situation 3: A Hispanic child announces, "When I growed up and be big, I'm gonna be white like you."

For each situation ask: What is the child's distorted thinking? How can you pay attention to the child's comment? How can you set a calm, relaxed atmosphere in which to discuss this concept? How can you affirm the child's thinking (without agreeing with the child?) How can you clarify the child's thinking (after making sure you understand the child?) How can you expand the child's thinking with some thought-provoking comments or questions?

Participants may wonder if they should provide all of these responses to a given situation. I would answer, *"No, but it is important to recognize all of the options and to increase our repertoire of responses."*

Critical Reflection: Responding to Children's Questions

30 minutes

Small Groups: What Were Your Questions?

Divide the class into small groups and ask them to reflect on their own childhood. Ask: What questions did you have about other cultures? How did the adults in your life respond to your questions? Then ask participants to think about children they have known. What questions about culture have children asked of you? How did you respond?

Mini-Lecture: Responding to Children's Questions

Present a mini-lecture briefly describing the four common responses to children's questions about differences and guidelines for responding. Refer to pages 200-201 in *Roots and Wings*.

Small Groups: Translating Responses

Ask participants to remain in their small groups. Distribute the handout "Responses to Children's Questions." This exercise gives participants an opportunity to translate common adult responses to children's questions about differences and culture. The objective is to identify one example of answering with a put-down, ignoring, using stereotypes, and giving accurate information. Tell the groups to complete the handout by reading each of the children's questions and writing one example of the four different responses to each question. Note: adult responses of ignoring may not involve the use of words. In this situation, participants can describe the adult's actions. For example: looks away, distracts child by saying, "Oh, look at this," grabs child by the hand and walks faster.

Responses to Children's Questions

Directions: Read each question. Discuss possible adult responses to the child's question. Write down one example for each type of adult response.

1. Yuck! Do they really eat that stuff?

   Put down _____

   Ignore them _____

   Stereotype _____

   Accurate information _____

2. What's that? (Child points to an Asian American child's eyes)

   Put down _____

   Ignore them _____

   Stereotype _____

   Accurate information _____

3. Why aren't his mom and dad the same?

   Put down _____

   Ignore them _____

   Stereotype _____

   Accurate information _____

4. Is she really an Indian? Is she gonna hurt me?

   Put down _____

   Ignore them _____

   Stereotype _____

   Accurate information _____

5. Does his color wash off?

   Put down _____

   Ignore them _____

   Stereotype _____

   Accurate information _____

6. Why does she talk funny?

   Put down _____

   Ignore them _____

   Stereotype _____

   Accurate information _____

Practical Application: Responding to Children's Discriminatory Behavior   **60 minutes**

Mini-Lecture: Responding Actively to Discriminatory Behavior

Present a mini-lecture on the strategies for responding to children's discriminatory behavior. Refer to pages 201-202 in *Roots and Wings*. You may want to post the guidelines, display them using an overhead projector, or make a handout of them. Participants may need to refer to the guidelines in the following activity.

Role Play: Now What Should I Do?

Divide the class into small groups of three to four participants. Ask them to create an incident around the topic of children's discriminatory behavior. One person needs to be the adult who responds to or interacts with the children. The situation does not need to be resolved, but rather, the small groups will present their situation as a problem to be solved by the entire class. Give the small groups 10 minutes to prepare their role play.

Have each group present their role play to the class. Then lead the class in analyzing the situation, using these questions to help the class to think about the role play.

1. What is the issue or problem?
2. What are the children feeling?
3. What is the adult feeling?
4. What do the children want and need?
5. What does the adult want and need?

Next, have the class brainstorm solutions and ask the small group to select three of the solutions they think might work. Have them test out the three solutions by role playing them for the class. Repeat until each small group has a chance to present and solve their situation.

Journaling

1. When have people discriminated against or been judgmental toward you? How did you feel? How did you respond?
2. Can you think of a time when a child made a discriminatory remark? How did you respond? How would you respond differently if a similar incident happened today? If so, what would you say and do?

Affirmations

Symbol: mouth
1. I embrace the power of words.
2. I clean up my own language by removing slang and derogatory words from my speech.
3. I find the courage within to speak out against injustice.
4. I empower myself by using words to express myself.

5. I affirm children's ethnic dialects and native languages.
6. I help children learn to verbally express themselves.
7. I use thoughtful comments and questions to help children expand their thinking.
8. I answer children's questions with simple accurate information.
9. I respond to children's discriminatory behavior.
10. I offer children understanding and forgiveness.
11. I am a role model to children with my speech and behavior.
12. I take advantage of teachable moments.
13. I welcome children's questions and interruptions.
14. I am flexible and spontaneous.
15. I speak from my innermost being about what is right and true.
16. I use my words and actions to show children that I care about respect, diversity, and equality.

Additional Activities

Role Play with Yourself

Here's role playing with a twist. Have the class identify situations related to talking with children about differences that teachers find difficult. Ask for volunteers to role play the situations. Only this time in the role play, have a class member play the part of the teacher's inner self (some may call this the inner voice or self-esteem). This inner self squats down behind the teacher and softly whispers the thoughts and feelings going on inside the teacher as she attempts to resolve the children's situation. This type of role play is very affirming, as it recognizes the feelings and inner thoughts teachers have as they go through their day.

Adapted from Virginia Satir. *The New Peoplemaking*. Mountain View, CA: Science and Behavior Books, Inc., 1988.

Communication Skills Checklist

Use the following checklist to help participants evaluate their communication skills related to talking to children about differences. Distribute a copy of the handout "Communication Skills for Talking to Children about Differences" to each participant. Ask them to read through the various types of responses and place a check mark in the left column if their parents used this technique in parenting them and a check mark in the right column if they currently use the technique in their classroom.

Ask participants to share the results with another person in the class and discuss these questions: How similar are your communication skills to those of your parents? Which skills did you learn from your parents? Which skills did you learn through training? Which skills did you learn on the job? Are there any skills on this list that you would like to incorporate into your teaching style? Which ones?

Communications Skills for Talking to Children about Differences

Directions: Read through this list of communications skills teachers use in talking to children about differences. Place a check mark in the left column if your parents used this communication method in parenting you. Place a check mark in the right-hand column if you currently use this communication method in teaching young children.

_____ **Name feelings.** "You look really sad, Juan. It hurt your feelings when Daniel called _____ you brown skin.' "

_____ **Express empathy.** "Gee, Damani, I know just how you feel. It hurts when people _____ call us names."

_____ **Voice your own feelings.** "I'm uncomfortable with the way you are playing _____ cowboys and Indians. I'm worried that you think Indians are bad guys and hurt people."

_____ **Respect the conflict and confusion.** "It's hard to use your words when you are _____ so upset."

_____ **Pay close attention** to children while they are talking. _____

_____ **Set a calm, relaxed atmosphere** so children have enough uninterrupted time in the _____ conversation to form and express their ideas.

_____ **Affirm the thinking.** "I believe you." _____

_____ **Clarify the thinking** by repeating the idea back to the child using some of their key _____ words and phrases.

_____ **Offer supportive, thought-provoking comments.** "Gee, that's an interesting _____ idea," "What makes you think that?"

_____ **Avoid evaluating children's ideas** by saying "good ideas" or "good solution." _____

_____ **Give accurate information.** "Yes, Pham's skin is darker than yours and his eyes _____ are shaped differently."

_____ **Protest.** "I don't like it when you call Marcus 'Blackie.' " _____

_____ **Describe the behavior you want.** "In our room we all play with one another. You _____ may choose who to play with but you may not leave someone out of your play because of how they look or how they talk."

_____ **Problem solve and set limits.** "Fabrizio wants to play with you again. If you two _____ play together, what will you need to feel safe?"

_____ **Do something.** "Mariah, I took the book you brought to school today off the shelf _____ because it has pictures of people that are untrue and unfair."

_____ **Encourage decision-making.** "Chidi, you can either play with Kamii or you can tell _____ her that you want to play with Sarah right now."

_____ **Encourage cooperation.** "What's going on?" "Hmmm, how can we work this out _____ so you are both happy?"

_____ **Tell children what you expect.** "Circle time is for our whole class to be together. _____ Everyone gets to be here in the circle."

_____ **Use visual displays.** Draw or cut out a picture of children playing Indians. With a _____ felt tip marker, draw a large "X" through it. Draw or cut out a picture of children playing together cooperatively. Put the two side-by-side for children to see.

Parent Interviews

As a class, plan to interview parents to find out how they talk to children about differences. Have the class brainstorm interview questions from the information in Chapter 9 of *Roots and Wings*. Create an interview questionnaire from the participants' questions. Assign each participant to interview five parents of young children and bring the results to the next class. Ask each participant to share results. Tabulate the results according to the types of responses outlined in *Roots and Wings*. Facilitate a large group discussion of the results by posing questions such as: What is the most common parental response? What is the least common parental response? What else do the results tell us?

Write a Newsletter Article

Ask participants to write an article for a parent newsletter or write a tip sheet for parents on how to talk to their children about differences.

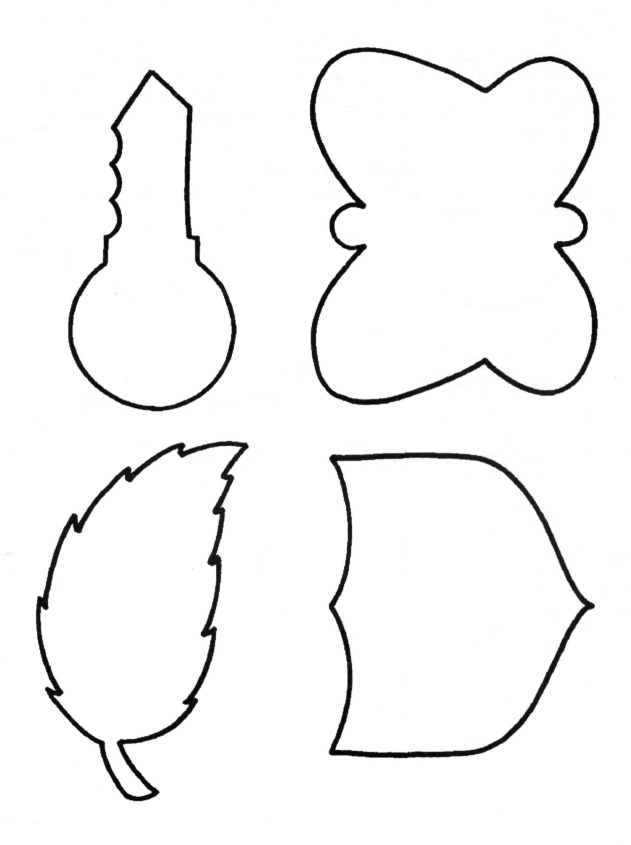

Bibliography

Aboud, Francis. *Children and Prejudice*. New York: Basil Blackwill, 1988.

Arnold, R., D. Barndt and Bev Burke. *A New Weave: Popular Education in Canada and Central America*. Toronto, Ontario: CUSO/Ontario Institute for Studies in Education, 1986.

Arnold, Rick and Bev Burke. *A Popular Education Handbook*. Toronto, Ontario: CUSO/Ontario Institute for Studies in Education, 1983.

Auvine, Brian, Betty Densmore, May Extrom, Scott Poole and Michel Shanklin. *A Manual for Group Facilitators*. Madison: The Center For Conflict Resolution, 1977.

Baker, Gwendolyn C. *Planning and Organizing for Multicultural Instruction*. Reading, MA: Addison-Wesley, 1983.

Bateman, Walter L. *Open to Question*. San Francisco: Jossey-Bass Publishers, 1990.

Belenky, Mary Field, Blythe McVicker Clinchy, Nancy Rule Goldberger, and Jill Mattuck Tarule. *Women's Ways of Knowing*. New York: Basic Books, Inc., 1986.

Brokering, Lois Redelfs. *Room to Grow*. Minneapolis: Augsburg Publishing House, 1988.

Capacchione, Lucia. *The Power of Your Other Hand*. North Hollywood, CA: Newcastle Publishing Co., 1988.

Carr, W. and S. Kemmis. *Becoming Critical: Education, Knowledge and Action Research*. Philadelphia: Farmer, 1986.

Coover, Virginia, Ellen Deacon, Charles Esser and Christopher Moore. *Resource Manual for A Living Revolution*. Philadelphia: New Society Publishers, 1977.

Derman-Sparks, Louise. *Anti-Bias Curriculum*. Washington D.C.: National Association for the Education of Young Children, 1989.

Derman-Sparks, Louise. *Anti-Bias Curriculum Video*. Pasadena: Pacific Oaks College, 1990.

Derman-Sparks, Louise, Carol Tanaka Higa and Bill Sparks. "Children, Race, and Racism: How Race Awareness Develops." *Interracial Books for Children Bulletin*, Vol. 11, 3 and 4. New York: Council on Interracial Books for Children, 1980.

Diamondstone, Jan M. *Designing, Leading and Evaluating Workshops for Teachers and Parents*. Ypsilanti, MI: High/Scope Foundation, 1980.

Edwards, Carolyn Pope. *Promoting Social and Moral Development in Young Children: Creative Approaches for the Classroom*. New York: Teachers College Press, 1986.

Evans, Alice Frazer, Robert A. Evans and William Bean Kennedy. *Pedagogies for the Non-Poor*. New York: Maryknoll, 1989.

Feeney, Stephanie, Doris Christensen and Eva Moravcik. *Who Am I in the Lives of Children?* Third edition. Columbus: Merrill, 1987.

Feeney, Stephanie and Robyn Chun. "Effective Teachers of Young Children." *Young Children*. (November 1985) 47-52.

Freire, Paulo and Ira Shor. *A Pedagogy for Liberation*. South Hadley, OH: Bergin and Garvey Publishers, 1987.

Freire, Paulo. *Education for Critical Consciousness*. New York: Continuum Publishing Corp., 1973.

____. *Pedagogy of the Oppressed*. New York: Continuum Publishing Corp., 1970.

____. *The Politics of Education*. South Hadley, OH: Bergin and Garvey Publishers, 1985.

Horton, Miles and Paulo Freire. *We Make the Road by Walking*. Philadelphia: Temple University Press, 1990.

Jones, Elizabeth. *Teaching Adults: An Active Learning Approach*. Washington D.C.: National Association for the Education of Young Children, 1986.

Katz, Judith H. *White Awareness: Handbook for Anti-Racism Training*. Norman, OK: University of Oklahoma Press, 1978.

Koberg, Don and Jim Bagnall. *The Revised All New Universal Traveler*. Los Altos: William Kaufman, 1981.

McGinnis, Kathleen. *Cultural Pluralism in Early Childhood Education*. St. Louis: Parish Board of Education, Lutheran Church, Missouri Synod, 1986.

McKay, Matthew, Martha Davis and Patrick Fanning. *Thoughts & Feelings: The Art of Cognitive Stress Intervention*. Richmond, CA: New Harbinger Publications, 1981.

Morgaine, Carol. "A Critical Theory of Self Formation." Ph.D. Thesis. University of Minnesota, 1990.

Morgaine, Carol. *Process Parenting: Breaking the Addictive Cycle*. St. Paul: Minnesota Department of Human Services, 1988.

Murdock, Maureen. *Spinning Inward*. Boston: Shambhala, 1987.

Newstrom, John W. and Edward E. Scannell. *Games Trainers Play*. New York: McGraw Hill Book Company, 1980.

Porter, Judith D.R. *Black Child, White Child: The Development of Racial Attitudes*. Cambridge: Harvard University Press, 1971.

Satir, Virginia. *The New Peoplemaking*. Mountain View, CA: Science and Behavior Books Inc., 1988.

Shor, Ira. *Critical Teaching and Everyday Life*. Chicago: University of Chicago Press, 1987.

____. *Freire for the Classroom*. Portsmouth: Boynton/Cook Publishers, 1987.

Steele, Shelby. *The Content of Our Character*. New York: St. Martin's Press, 1990.

Williams, Leslie R. and Yvonne DeGaetano. *Alerta: A Multicultural, Bilingual Approach to Teaching Young Children*. Menlo Park: Addison-Wesley, 1985.

Vanderslice, Virginia, Florence Cherry, Moncrieff Cochran and Christiann Dean. *Communication for Empowerment*. Ithaca: Cornell University, 1984.

von Oech, Roger. *Creative Whack Pack*. Stamford, CT: U.S. Games Systems, Inc., 1989.

York, Stacey L. *Roots and Wings: Affirming Culture in Early Childhood Programs*. St. Paul: Redleaf Press, 1991.